THEATRE AND STAGE SERIES

General Editor: HAROLD DOWNS

THE CRITIC IN THE THEATRE

THE CRITIC IN THE THEATRE

BY

HAROLD DOWNS

WITH A FOREWORD BY

NEVILLE CARDUS

LONDON
SIR ISAAC PITMAN & SONS, LTD.

First published 1953

SIR ISAAC PITMAN & SONS, Ltd.
PITMAN HOUSE, PARKER STREET, KINGSWAY, LONDON, W.C.2
THE PITMAN PRESS, BATH
PITMAN HOUSE, LITTLE COLLINS STREET, MELBOURNE
27 BECKETTS BUILDINGS, PRESIDENT STREET, JOHANNESBURG

ASSOCIATED COMPANIES
PITMAN PUBLISHING CORPORATION
2 WEST 45TH STREET, NEW YORK
SIR ISAAC PITMAN & SONS (CANADA), Ltd.
(INCORPORATING THE COMMERCIAL TEXT BOOK COMPANY)
PITMAN HOUSE, 381–383 CHURCH STREET, TORONTO

MADE IN GREAT BRITAIN AT THE PITMAN PRESS, BATH
E3—(G.437)

"The golden rule is that there are no golden rules."

GEORGE BERNARD SHAW:
"Maxims for Revolutionists" (*Man and Superman*)

FOREWORD

I DON'T know of any book on the theatre quite like this of Mr. Downs. A whole library can easily be compiled dealing with plays, the interpretation of them, their construction and technique; with actors and acting; with producers, stagecraft, and scene-shifters, and "all the rest of it." But this surely is the first time the dramatic critic has received the honour and the charity of discussion, analysis, and justification in a volume devoted entirely to his job and his point of view.

Charity, of course, should more or less begin at home; and Mr. Downs in these pages reveals himself an experienced critic of the theatre and of all who serve the dramatist's purpose. He brings not only experience to each chapter, but a well-stocked mind. If at the end he may not convince everybody who has suffered under criticism that the practitioners of it possess stronger "right" to an opinion than any of their praise-singing friends, well—that is neither here nor there.

Myself I have learned much, or have found on several pages an aspect of criticism emphasized which I have in my own avenue of criticism often neglected. Should a critic go beyond accounting for the way his mind has received a play (or any other creative work) aesthetically? Is he qualified to tell the producer where he has, in the critic's opinion, gone wrong? As a music critic I have never, even in my most lofty *Manchester Guardian* years, dreamed of offering a Schnabel or a Toscanini or a Flagstad—let alone a Strauss—technical advice. The main thing was to get imaginatively into the heart of a work and performance and then to describe, in as good and suggestive English as one could command, an experience of mind and spirit while under the creator's spell. This is merely one way—it has been called the way of the "sensitized plate." But it is an error to think that such a way denotes indifference to hard study, logical analysis, and some acquaintance with the best that has been achieved in all schools. The "sensitized plate" critic prepares himself, cultivates himself until he develops antennae or "cat's whiskers" which he trusts to work instinctively when he surrenders temporarily to the creative artist. It is a case, with him, of love and faith as much as of deliberately directed reason. He is, in a word, merely one of the audience—but more enlightened, more expert at reception (because this is his livelihood) than the rest. The trouble with the dominant school of criticism today is that the tendency is towards analysis before the imagination has been allowed the chance to make a synthesis.

Mr. Downs touches on all schools—from the critic who apropos of Shakespeare talks of himself to the hard-pressed hack who late at night has to telephone a "helpful" "informative" paragraph. Like any other good book it stimulates as much as it establishes and defines.

NEVILLE CARDUS

PREFACE

STATISTICS, sometimes uninteresting and often repellent to average people, are, from time to time, significant even when they are not essential.

A census of theatres taken towards the close of the first half of the twentieth century—during 1948 to be exact—produced the following statistical information—

London Theatres	62
London Suburban Theatres and Music Halls .	22
Provincial Theatres and Music Halls . .	168
Provincial Repertory Theatres . . .	150
	402

During the same year the total of amateur dramatic and operatic societies that were affiliated to national organizations was between 8,000 and 9,000.

The exact total of theatregoers during 1948 is unknown. Anyone who is interested can make an estimate. What is certain is that each theatregoer had her or his opinion on the theatrical entertainment that was seen and judged. The experts agreed—or differed—among themselves. So, too, did the theatregoers. Harmonies, differences of opinion, and discords are expressions of life itself. Human beings differ because they think differently; act as individuals because they are individuals. Differences are of greater value in human life than would be a flat monotony of enduring uniformity; which, fortunately, is not within the scope of human attainment.

Dramatic and theatrical entertainment, from a five-fold angle—play-writing, producing, acting, theatregoing, and criticizing—is the subject of this volume. Its treatment is intended to provoke discussion, to which end persisting issues are re-stated and new problems, of importance to all who are interested in theatregoing, introduced.

Many attempts that are made to discipline and to dragoon people should be the signals for revolt. Men and women take—or can take—within limitations their recreative pleasures as, and where, they will. They may neither receive the commendation of friends nor the approval of critics, but they express their lives in their own ways. Comment, praise, and criticism, based on imaginative understanding, toleration, and judicious impartiality, are moulding influences that are always at work.

HAROLD DOWNS

CONTENTS

xi

CHAPTER I

THE CRITIC'S FUNCTION

DURING nearly half a century's theatregoing I have heard, between the acts in the theatre or on leaving it to re-enter the world of practical affairs outside, many casual remarks which were dramatic criticism in embryo.

Criticism is, in part, comparison, and theatregoers for their appraisement draw spontaneously upon knowledge that is readily to hand. By their overheard conversation in foyer, bar, or auditorium they unwittingly inform any within hearing-range of their likes and dislikes, their prejudices and partialities.

What these expressive theatregoers say during a performance, between the acts, and after the final curtain, is their "dramatic criticism," of a comedy or a tragedy, a farce or a "musical"; in short, of any form of theatrical entertainment they have enjoyed, or failed to enjoy.

I was at the first night of J. B. Priestley's ambitiously experimental play, *Johnson Over Jordan*, at the New Theatre, on 22nd February, 1939. The playwright in his essay "And All About It," given in the printed version of the play, "Dedicated with thanks and good wishes to all who shared with me this adventure of the theatre," explains what he had in mind when he wrote the play. I quote his words because in sound dramatic criticism one essential is that the critic in the theatre should see clearly and understand thoroughly the author's intention.

"Actually, what I wanted to do was to give an account, in dramatic form, of a man's life in a new way, taking an ordinary middle-class citizen of our time and then throwing a new light on him and his affairs, and giving to my record of his rather commonplace life an unusual depth and buoyancy."[1]

The author's intention was evidently missed by the two young men who, in my hearing as we were leaving the theatre, peremptorily dismissed the play in a few words.

[1] *Johnson Over Jordan.*

"I don't see what he's driving at," said one.

"It's highfalutin rubbish," commented the other.

The two proceeded to discuss, with relish, a light comedy they had seen a few nights before.

It is true that *Johnson Over Jordan* met with what is called "an unfavourable Press," to which the printed version refers: ". . . the play had been taken off, on 6th May, 1939. As soon as we announced the final performance there was the same rush to the box office and we had packed houses. We were implored to keep it on, and the theatre management offered to run it at their own risk, but we felt that we could not change our minds again. The many letters I have recently received convince me that for once it is true that a hostile or stupid press badly damaged a play's chances. Nor did we ever succeed in capturing the interest of the well-to-do play-going public. (From first to last our cheaper seats were filled.)"

Sometimes the casual or critical remarks of theatregoers are concerned with production or players rather than with the play itself.

On the first night of *Rose Marie* at Drury Lane on 20th March, 1925, I had with me a Welsh author, a Shakespearean scholar, and a keen lover of classical music, whose favourite composer was Bach. He was, he told me a number of times during the evening, "bored, so damned bored," most of all by one of the repetitive "hits" of the production, and he waited impatiently for the final curtain.

Also bored was the blasé Oxford undergraduate who accompanied me to the Apollo Theatre on 11th October, 1929, to see the first performance of Sean O'Casey's *The Silver Tassie*, the second act of which, with its expressionism, plus its stylized mounting and dressing, caused him to state his preference for "something straightforward and to the point."

At the first night of *The Dancing Years*, produced by Leontine Sagan, which had its first performance at Drury Lane on 23rd March, 1939, a woman professional colleague who was with me had in mind *Glamorous Night* (1935), *Careless Rapture* (1936), and *Crest of the Wave* (1937) as she pronounced judgment in staccato—"typical Novello." She called herself a "Novello fan," and was appreciative, without qualifications or defensive explanations, although not so much an ardently-recurring supporter of this dramatic-author-composer's works as was K. O. Newman of one particular play. A man with an extraordinary, perhaps a unique, experience, Mr. Newman wrote[1]—

"I took great interest in a play, written by a friend of mine, and produced by another one, and followed it through its various stages from the original typescript, attending rehearsals and the first five months of its run.

"See a play once; a few plays more than once; and the majority of plays never: undeterred by this charter of theatrical attendance I decided for unreasonable action. I could therefore neither ask for nor expect sympathy from anybody. So much was clear to me at the outset.

"I went to the theatre as to an office and never broke the sequence of my attendances. Matinée or evening performance, rain or shine, found me in my seat. The latter half of the first twenty-five performances was perhaps the most trying period. Then I got my second wind. I learned to sleep, open-eyed, through the more irksome passages of the play."

He saw it 250 times!

Bernard Shaw's written comment to the author on learning of this persistent theatregoer in action was: "I don't know what to say about this book. The experience on which it is founded is so extraordinary that an honest record of it should be preserved. But it would have driven me mad; and I am not sure that the author came out of it without a slight derangement."

Early Experiences

My introduction to the theatre was made in a small market town where my brother took me to see *The Bells*, performed by a visiting company in what was locally termed "the threepenny gaff," a structure of wood and canvas. He paid threepence for my seat, a width of about twelve inches on a piece of board about four inches across, which made a trestle-like form.

When "the gaff" first opened, the floor was of grass, the heating and lighting were by an improvised installation, and

---

[1] *Two Hundred and Fifty Times I Saw a Play.*

there was a two-player orchestra—a pianist and a violinist. When they began to play the house lights were down; so, too, was the curtain, but the "footlights" were "on."

I was young, too young to know anything of the theatre, but its romantic spirit, even in these crude circumstances, fired my imagination, which, ever since, has been stimulated, though never with like intensity, by the artificiality of the theatre. Even the attenuated "orchestra" created pleasurable expectancy. My brother, noting this, turned to assure me: "This isn't all you've come to see."

Soon the truth of his remark was reinforced by what to me then was the strange traffic of the stage, the impression made on my boyish mind probably being deeper than that which was made on more mature minds by Henry Irving at the Lyceum in 1871, or by Frederick Valk on my mind in the 1950 revival at Camden Town's Bedford Theatre. This revival, incidentally, created the opportunity for one critic in the theatre (*The Times*, 30th May, 1950) to re-write an interesting episode in the history of Irving, *The Bells*, and melodrama—

"We are told there are people who have not seen Irving in *The Bells*, and we find it hard to believe. The experience worked over by pen and pencil with such vivid results has become one of our inherited playgoing memories. It would be unfair, nevertheless, to use the memories of 1870 against Mr. Frederick Valk, except to note that he does not choose to follow in the Irving tradition.

"*Le Juif Polonais*, as played by Coquelin, was the realistic study of an unimaginative little murderer chuckling with self-satisfaction at having hoodwinked his neighbours and cheated the law. *The Bells* differed from the Erckmann-Chatrian play in little but its stage directions, but into it Irving read the Manfredesque horrors of a conscience tortured by guilt. He played Mathias as a man accursed; Mr. Valk— appearing to follow the text logically and correctly—plays him as a man who would be perfectly content to enjoy his ill-gotten gains but for the untimely repetition in his ears of the sound of the Polish Jew's sleigh bells, a physical *malaise* rather than an intolerable materialization of spiritual torment. Irving,

according to our memories, was a mind in torment; Mr. Valk
is merely a malefactor brought to justice by an improbable
concatenation of events.

"It makes all the difference; and it would be idle to pretend
that the old melodrama stands up to this kind of revival. Mr.
Valk is a powerful actor, the best Solness of our time and a
remarkably fine Borkman, and, as was to be expected, he has
some impressive moments when Mathias is tried for his life in
his dream; but it cannot be said that he brings this historic
melodrama to life, it cannot be said that he revives memories
either of Irving or of Coquelin."

This gem of criticism should be specially noted now in view
of what is later stated to be the function of the critic in the
theatre, who, drawing upon special and extensive knowledge
and applying it, delivers his appraisals of plays.

During the stay of "the gaff" I spent nothing on sweets or
on any of the things that appeal to boys, and all my pocket-
money went on theatregoing, with the result that when the
company left I had also seen *East Lynne, The Face at the Window,
Sweeney Todd, The Colleen Bawn, Maria Marten,* and other
"classics" in the repertoire.

My brother not only introduced me to the theatre, but also
helped me to cultivate the theatregoing habit. Every Saturday
he travelled twenty miles to Leeds, where he tried to see every
musical comedy. He had a quick ear. Every Sunday I sang,
as usual, as a chorister at morning and evening services in
Selby Abbey, and listened to him during the afternoon as he
"tried out" the popular numbers that he had heard and
memorized the night before, sometimes aided by a cheaply
printed sheet of "all the popular songs."

These superficial details serve as reminders that adolescents
and adults who go to the theatre react to what they see on and
hear from the stage, and give expression to their reactions.

When children are taken to the theatre, it is easily seen
whether they are bored or entertained. The theatregoing of
adolescents and adults is selective. They pay for theatre seats
for a variety of reasons, and, irrespective of the verdicts of
the critics in the theatre, whose serious criticism they may
never hear or read, say what they think of the theatrical

entertainment that costs them money. What they say does not necessarily constitute sound criticism!

Theatregoing creates unexpected and pleasurable surprises, and leads to disappointments, deserved or undeserved. What is experienced depends to some extent upon expectations of what an individual thinks the theatre should provide; what he has a right to demand; what kind of value he hopes for in return for his expenditure of money and time.

There has been movement since those Puritan days when the theatre was thought of as the devil's playhouse, with or without the concomitant association of actors and actresses as rogues and vagabonds, but there lingers in some minds, possibly influenced by theological conceptions, the idea that theatregoing should be renounced, if not denounced.

I have known residents in cathedral cities who would pay an occasional visit to the theatre as a social event, but who would not go during Holy Week, which remains one of the worst business weeks of the year in the world of the theatre.

Until two or three years ago I had a theatregoing friend who ostentatiously walked out of the theatre if the dialogue of any play introduced a direct reference to or specific mention of the Deity. Today my friends include devout churchgoers who as spasmodic theatregoers will not support the works of playwrights who discuss, freely and in "the modern spirit," sex and theological themes.

Commercial enterprise has transformed, if not entirely eliminated, "the threepenny gaff," but modern theatres, when compared with modern cinemas, are relatively few, and extensive regions of the country are now without "legitimate" theatres. Whether the community needs the creative literary or dramatic artist is an issue that has been debated through the ages, and whether rural England can create or adequately support a drama of its own is an interesting problem that has yet to be solved. One specialist on the subject, Bernard Gilbert, has written[1]—

"The first thirty years of my life were spent in a village, and in that period I heard no music later than Mendelssohn, saw no plays more intellectual than Gilbert and Sullivan, and met

[1] *King Lear at Hordle and Other Rural Plays.*

only one man who had the slightest interest in literature. The entertainments which were given to us on winter evenings can only be described as vapid. Drama was always popular, and probably the peasant can receive art in this manner more easily than in any other. . . .

"We wanted Drama, however, more than anything else.

"I was already acquainted with Shaw, Ibsen, and Sudermann, and beginning to feel a strong inclination to produce *Candida*. At this point an enthusiast from the nearest market-town came with a company of amateurs, and gave a musical play which delighted everybody. 'But why don't you give us something *good*?' said I; at which he smiled. 'Your village doesn't want what you call *good* plays,' he said. 'It would hate them, and in any case, you have your cast to consider.' 'All right,' said I, 'then why not do some of the little folk plays of Synge or Tolstoy?' But he had never heard of either, and the discussion meandered into the desert. . . . There was no difficulty, either, about production, because the blacksmith, the cobbler, the carpenter's daughter, etc., all acted their own parts, wherein they had nothing to do but behave and speak exactly as they would under the given circumstances. . . .

"Until modern methods of transport were devised and modern means of communication began to be widely applied, rural areas were studded with isolated settlements, with villages which had little or no effective contact either with their neighbours or with the towns and cities which for practical purposes might have been hundreds instead of tens of miles away. But the telephone, wireless, the cinema, and the travelling theatre as exemplified by the admirable work that has been done by such organizations as the Arts League of Service, and amateur bodies, have revolutionized life in the rural areas."

The Theatre's Firm Hold

Although both rural areas and many urban areas remain without a "legitimate" theatre many years after the above passage was written (1922) and notwithstanding new changes that have been made possible by science—television, for example— the theatre retains a firm hold on a minority of those who seek recreative-cultural entertainment. It also continues to be an irresistible attraction for a larger number of people who lack selective ability, their inescapable minimum requirement, not always met, being that they must be entertained. Once inside the theatre they become participators in a common experience and susceptible to collective influences; indeed, they are much more sensitive in the environment of the artificial world that they have entered for the fulfilment of their pleasure-seeking than are the critics in the theatre who fight against superficial and stultifying sophistication.

Years ago Romain Rolland wrote a book and fell foul of the critics. One, recalling some of the difficulties that confront the creators of a theatre for the people, remarked: "He (Romain Rolland) is undeterred by the fact that a dozen other reformers before him have attempted to impose the same severe regimen upon 'the people and have failed'." Rolland wanted "tragic plays that exalt the heroic powers of the soul, the vigour of its passions and of its will." His "theatre of the people" was to set before the people the spectacle of heroic virtues, and so stimulate them to heroic action. That was the ideal of Rousseau. The French theatre, like the Greek, was to present "grave and superb spectacles . . . showing forth only combats, victories, prizes, objects capable of inspiring the ardent emulation and of kindling the heart with sentiments of honour and glory." Mercier, in 1773 and 1778, laid it down that the first duty of the dramatist was "to mould the manners and morals of his fellow-citizens." For Chénier (1789) the theatre was "a means of public instruction." The leading spirits of the Revolution planned a national theatre that should make the people better by setting before them the spectacle of the heroic past, or of the Revolution itself; Boissy d'Anglas looked to the theatre to make men "more virtuous and enlightened." Michelet, in later days, wanted "to nourish the people with the people" by showing them "their own legends, their own deeds." The people, apparently, did not want to be made more heroic and more virtuous: the Committee of Public Safety did not succeed in establishing its new moral theatre permanently.

It seems that what was attempted more than a century-and-a-half ago is still being attempted, with variations and modifications!

I have quoted authors who have had a special interest in the theatre, but have not necessarily been of it. Do the opinions of those with a long working experience gained within the theatre itself differ? In detail, but not, basically, in principle and in mental attitude.

Inasmuch as all people who go to the theatre for entertainment go with an open and receptive mind, it may be said that the mental attitude of all is more or less similar as soon as they become part of an audience in the theatre.

George Arliss in his autobiography (*George Arliss by Himself*) contended that the art of the actor is appreciated more by one person than another; that the story is the chief consideration with practically everyone; and that the primitive in human beings remains unchanged through the ages. These contentions, expressed by one who had long and intimate personal experience of the traffic of the stage, draw special attention to man in his simple and material states.

Another worker in the theatre, Theodore Komisarjevsky, induces reflection on Man on a different plane of functioning:[1] "The theatre offers the spectator not alone relief from the routine of his everyday, humdrum existence, but develops him spiritually and leads him forward. The theatre is the place where people have always gone to understand themselves, to share their griefs and joys with others, where they felt as a People and not as a crowd of solitary entities. . . .

"At all times when the theatre mattered as an institution of culture and as an expression of the pioneer spirit of humanity, the work of its artists was dedicated to the problems of the relationship of man to man, to spiritual, social, political and psychological questions treated in an emotional, stimulating form and illuminated with the light of transcendental knowledge."

It is easy to get the theatre in focus, but seemingly impossible for all who focus attention upon it to reach unanimity. In this, as in many aspects of life and its expression, there is no Absolute. The individual spirit, mind, and body remain supreme.

Each human being functions on an individual level.

[1] *The Theatre.*

Doubtless, there are numerous other human beings whose development is similar, whose level is on a par with that of any one of millions, but there is no irresistible magnet that brings all together at one time in one place for only one identical purpose.

Any audience in any theatre is a composite whole, but the persons of whom it is constituted, although reflectors of common characteristics, are not identical. One section may be a party that is having a night out at the theatre. Isolated individuals will be present—one to kill time, another to see a specific play, another to renew acquaintance with a "star" actor or actress, another to indulge theatregoing as a social habit, another for a business reason, another to express cultural tastes, another to relieve boredom, another to find spiritual solace, another to partake of intellectual food, another to experience the satisfaction of the release of pent-up emotions, another to be amused by the reflection of everyday life in action, another to give expression to the gregarious instinct that impels people to assemble at one place at the same time for one primary and numerous secondary purposes: exactitude would necessitate a greatly extended and detailed enumeration of the reasons why people go to the theatre.

These glancing suggestions, however, are sufficient to bring into perspective the difficulty of the task of the critic in the theatre. He, too, is an individual—but different from most of the individuals who constitute any theatre audience. He takes with him as part of his indispensable equipment special knowledge acquired systematically as a specialist-student and added to by practical experience. He has become facile, if not always felicitous, in his professional application of that knowledge. His considered opinions are his own, but they are, in a sense, qualified. He, too, is affected by environment, but to a slight degree only in comparison with the readily impressionable casual theatregoer who is in the theatre to be amused and entertained. He is also a servant, though not a slave. His published criticism is the crystallization of his opinions on play, production, and performance. He can be, perhaps is, an individual without any obligation to meet in his written expressions the requirements of others. Yet he writes under a

self-imposed restraint born of his consciousness not only of
what his newspaper or periodical proprietor or editor expects
of him, but also of what some theatregoers will look for in his
considered judgment on the play which they have paid to see
and which he himself has been paid to see and to deal with as
a professional critic in the theatre.

He is, however, more than a professional critic and more
than an individual. He is a human being with some of the
weaknesses, foibles, prejudices, preferences, and convictions
that are inherent—even in the most highly integrated man or
woman. He strives to maintain impartiality—and from time
to time fails. He has his own idiosyncracies, and sometimes
prevents them from seeping into his written expressions, but
sometimes they are there—blemishes that mar. He may be
prejudiced against certain forms of theatrical entertainment,
and have personal preferences. He has convictions that are
founded on a reasoned acceptance of first principles, but
modifies the assertion of them now and again, even if, for
expediency's sake, he does not permit himself to become an
opportunist.

Mr. T. C. Worsley, reviewing (*The New Statesman and Nation*,
26th July, 1952) a particularly challenging treatment of the
contemporary theatre, by Richard Findlater,[1] pointed out
that the interest of the author's approach "comes from his
being himself, I fancy, in a stage of mental and political
transition. His fluid present is always contradicting his rigid
past. If it were letters that he were discussing, he might
possibly still be left-wing, *avant-garde*. But it is less easy to
discuss the theatre academically. There the theoretical is
constantly being brought up with a bump against stubborn
realities. The audience is one of these—predominantly out for
a distracting evening and comfortably unadvanced; and you
cannot, except by a sublime act of faith, disregard the audience
entirely. If you do, you may land in O'Casey's predicament
which Mr. Findlater neatly summarizes—it is a fair sample of
his approach—

> He is writing plays for a working-class audience that does not
> exist, for a people's theatre that lives only in his mind, and

[1] *The Unholy Trade.*

moreover he is blowing his trumpet outside a Jericho whose walls have long since collapsed. He is writing revolutionary plays about Ireland, and about an ideal Ireland at that, for an audience of English trades unionists in the Welfare State. He is attacking the buried morality of the Victorian age, preaching the doctrine of revolution by the strike, challenging with a sense of real defiance the Lord Jehovah.''

Like the creative literary artist, he reflects in his writing some of the spirit of the times in which he writes, and, like the revolutionary poet who is disregardful of the impact of his imaginative work on established institutions, he thinks and looks ahead, theorizing in order to bring the probable future into the known present.

Mirror and Recorder

Theatrical tastes change with the changing world. The contemporary theatre is both a mirror and a recorder. It reflects the daily interests and activities of people who are often primarily concerned with the performance of the essential tasks of earning a living. It registers many of the conflicts that arise in the material transactions of everyday life and clarifies, enriches, and intensifies spiritual aspirations.

When drama was rooted in the Church it was religious and didactic. Then, the purposes of the theatre, religious purposes, were different from its purposes in these secular days of the twentieth century. Inevitable, too, is the difference in the tastes of theatregoers of today when comparison is struck between these and those of their Restoration, Elizabethan, and earlier predecessors. None the less, the entertainment value that is inherent in theatrical work-play remains.

The theatre is a man-made institution, and the human contributions that are made to it affect it in various ways. The playwright, thinking retrospectively, may write in reaction from what has happened, proceed to record what is, and suggest what may be: his intention, in short, is unlikely to be static throughout his own lifetime. The player's performance and its relative values do not remain fixed and immutable. Playwrights, as creative artists, write in response to the creative urge, and what they write influences not only what, but how, players act. Directors or producers, whose aims and emphases change with the passing of time, also exert influences on tastes and fashions. Shakespeare "created" the part of Hamlet. Since its creation many actors have "created" and "interpreted." Which actor has given us the "best Hamlet" of this century? The question—fatuous no doubt—if asked, can be provocative, and the answers that can be returned to it can be stimulating, but any aesthetic value arising from the question and the answers is likely to be negligible. The "part," like the whole, was written by Shakespeare. Explanations of what has been done with it, and why, since it was "created" by the playwright are some of the raw material that must be drawn upon by any narrator who would write the history of playwriting, play production, and play acting. The "part" has many facets and can have many different interpretations. Is there only one interpretation that is "right?"—the question is intended to brush aside man's unending pursuit of Perfection.

The critic in the theatre needs to be keenly aware of the possibilities of legitimate differences in the appraisements of the playwright's aims, of the producer's opinions of what is desirable or necessary in communicating, through the players, the content of a play to the audience, and of the richly varied scope that is presented to the players (with the "permission," on occasions, of the director or producer to exercise their powers of interpretation through portrayal). The presentation, in totality, needs to be virile and convincing alike for, in purpose and degree, the very real life outside the theatre must be transferred to the theatre and there transmuted but not so that touch with reality is lost.

The critic in the theatre cannot concern himself wholly with playwright, play, and players. He is a member of the audience and aware of marked differences between himself and the majority of the theatregoers with whom he is temporarily associated.

Both consciously and subconsciously he is affected by his environment. "Money," contends R. D. Charques,[1] "rules in the theatre as in no other art—except, of course, the cinema, which is frankly conducted as an industry; and it is this fact which gives a fatal twist to the theatre's creative potentialities.

---

[1] *Contemporary Literature and Social Revolution.*

For the thing that brings a performance to life in the theatre and creates the illusion of reality is the wave of sympathy and collaboration between audience and actor, the strange flow of intimacy between the people on one side of the footlights and the people on the other. Without that intimate reciprocal relation there is no consciousness of drama, no act of creation in the theatre."

The sincerely-held opinions of the critic in the theatre are often at variance with those of the casual theatregoer. Sincerity is the keynote of his writing as a critic, but he recognizes the necessity to serve the public, through his newspaper or periodical, as a reporter. Then he deduces what he thinks are the reactions of the audience to the theatrical entertainment provided on the stage. Yet as he theorizes and reports he is aware of the impossibility of working out his theories and systematizing the bases of his criticism through each individual's attitude, which is an amalgam of the results produced by the play and the players on imagination, mind, and emotions.

Although no two human beings in the theatre are identical in all respects, there are numerous similarities that express themselves in collective reactions and manifestations. These are registered by the critic in the theatre, who is sensitive to them but not necessarily to the point at which he *must* incorporate their effects directly into his writing.

What is the critic's function? What should be the purpose of dramatic criticism? It is certain that the critic in the theatre must be concerned with play, production, performance, and audience.

CHAPTER II

THE CRITIC'S BASES OF COMPARISON

THE attitude of the average theatregoer towards theatre-going is sharply differentiated from that of the critic in the theatre. There are similarities, but, basically, their expectations are different.

Although "the average theatregoer" as a descriptive phrase comes readily to mind, any attempt to define him (or her) in precise terms that can be applied both extensively and with complete accuracy meets with frustration.

Any one of many reasons for theatregoing can be related to the average theatregoer and his intentions. The probability, however, is that those reasons that have a bearing on the deliberate search for pleasurable entertainment will be nearest to a true explanation. In many instances, the search will, indeed, be casual rather than deliberate; or, perhaps, still nearer the mark is the statement that a visit to the theatre now and again is the outcome of the desire to spend two or three hours with an audience that has assembled for the specific purpose of being amused. The accent is on results. Analytical thought will not have been exercised previously in order to apply scientifically a selective principle. Primary concern will not have been about the material that the actors and actresses work upon, but about the effects that they are reported to be able to create, or the anticipation of effects that can be expected from previous knowledge of "stars" or rank-and-file players.

It is true that the average theatregoer who is correctly placed in a specific category will not have reached his decision to go to the theatre without any thought whatever. Some theatregoers eschew tragedy in all circumstances. For them a tragedy is an insuperable barrier, a persisting taboo. These theatregoers, however, may very well be some of the most enthusiastic and regular supporters of comedy, or biographical or historical plays, or "musicals" or revue. The average theatregoer, in short, is as varied in his hopes, desires, demands, and requirements as is the average seeker of entertainment of any kind, or the average exponent of the art of living in any sphere. He is in a position to act—and he does act—in harmony with his preferences, but these can be so highly individualized as to strike hard at the soundness of dogmatic generalizations.

It is best to acknowledge the uniqueness of each individual. And it is practical to recognize that, for diverse reasons, hundreds of human beings, each on an individual plane, have become members of an audience, in order to see and to hear the presentation of theatrical entertainment and in the hope that expectations will be pleasurably realized.

The professional critic, on the other hand, must go to the theatre, perhaps three, four, or more times during one week, for purposes that are obvious—not always what they should be—if they are to be in accord with the sound application of principles of criticism. He, too, has his preferences.

The average professional critic is as hard to define as is the average theatregoer.

Fortuitous occupational circumstances may have turned him into a critic in the theatre at a time when he was unable to exercise a genuine option to be professionally someone quite different from a professional critic. He may have graduated from general writing to specialized criticism in accordance with clearly conceived professional aims. He may have realized these so well that he finds himself able to make adequate use of his special knowledge. At the same time, he may reveal and demonstrate aptitude and ability as an interpreter and an appraiser of plays in performance. Further, theatregoers may recognize in his criticism the clarification and elaboration of their own nebulous ideas and jostling opinions that lack a solid foundation.

The professional critic at best is one who not only knows the story of the evolution of Drama, but also its significant impact, through the theatre, on theatregoers, and its influences, direct or indirect, on dramatic literature. The professional critic at worst is less easily defined. He is certainly to be numbered with those who abuse a privileged position, who are unmindful of basic values, and who deal, superficially and insincerely, with the collective work and activities that bring to life dramatic and theatrical material that the average theatregoer has paid to see and to hear.

Both the professional critic who is an expert in sound criticism and the mere pseudo-critic-intruder in the world of the theatre find it necessary to be more catholic in taste, more open-minded, more tolerant, readier to search for the playwright's purpose, than the average theatregoer needs to be, for the critic or the intruder is engaged professionally or occupationally while the other is more likely to be on pleasure bent than in pursuit of cultural profit, which is not, however, ruled out as a possibility.

In individual cases there may be opportunities for the transference of professional obligations. The late James Agate was a brilliant critic in the theatre, with strong preferences and equally strong prejudices. As a critic he was called upon to deal with the traffic of the stage, but, on occasions, he deliberately dodged some of the traffic by throwing the onus of evaluation on one of his colleagues, realizing that because of his preferences and prejudices alike he was as likely, in sincerity, to be unjust as to be impartial, niggardly rather than generous in praise and appreciation because of his strong distastes or deep-rooted convictions. It is not surprising, in these circumstances, that some of his best criticism was concerned with classical drama, with Shakespeare, with plays of the Elizabethan and Restoration ages, with the most significant contributions to modern drama, and not with theatrical pieces that are manufactured rather than created to please noncritical and easily satisfied theatregoers.

I realize, however, that I am not strictly correct in so describing the theatregoers whose theatrical tastes are far different from those that were enjoyed by Mr. Agate. He did not place musical comedy at the top of dramatic and theatrical entertainment on his list of comparative values. Theatregoers whose first choice in this connexion is musical comedy are not necessarily non-critical or easily satisfied. These theatregoers, too, have strong preferences and strong prejudices, and within their own spheres of choice are capable of striking comparisons which, in effect, are pertinent criticisms.

Few professional critics in the theatre, however, are able to choose the plays upon which they will pronounce professional judgment. Their professional status places them under the obligation to see all types of plays, varied dramatic and theatrical entertainment, and to exercise their critical faculty upon them, excepting those "dramatic critics" who are not critics, but reporters, gossip-writers, or story-tellers. Their function is to provide newspaper readers with matter that romanticizes the actual, panders to human curiosity and innate snobbery, and makes for dilettantism.

The Critic's Range of Knowledge

What, then, should be the range of knowledge of the critic in the theatre?

Must he have mastered the alphabet of the history of drama? Know the order of the chapters in its evolution? Be expert in assessing the respective values of the drama of his own country compared with the drama of France or of America, or of Germany, Norway, Italy, or any other country in western civilization? Must he be able to strike comparisons between the civilization of which we are members and civilizations that have gone? Be familiar with the details of practical and dramatic activities that are "encouraged" by totalitarian states?

These questions, intended to be indicative, are certainly not comprehensive.

The replies may be grouped in the generalization—the critic in the theatre, to be worthy of his status, must have knowledge of the origins and the developments of his special subjects, drama and theatre. Will, then, acquisition of this specialized knowledge be followed by adequate scope for its application in published criticism? Do modern journalistic practices and the methods of present-day publishing create the conditions under which the specialist can make the fullest use of his specialization? The answers are "No" repeated, but the negative can be qualified with advantage.

Is it worth while to know quite a lot of what can be known in order to feel that confidence which comes from mastery? This time the answer is a direct "Yes," which, however, can also be qualified. In philosophic caution, the approach can be prefaced by the phrase "it all depends"—and the dependence waits upon circumstance.

When a young man who was interested in criticism and who wanted to know how to "become a dramatic critic" asked Mr. Agate for advice, he received an illuminating, if challenging, reply. It was:[1] "It all depends upon the type of paper you are aiming at. If you want to write in the popular Press about schoolgirls turning themselves into star-actresses overnight—which is what that institution understands as dramatic criticism—then you should waylay some popular editor in his favourite night haunt, and impress him with your knowledge of the private lives of crooners, insinuate that you hold Shakespeare to be a back number, Tchehov a dud, and Shaw an irresponsible pantaloon. Let him glean that you write even more vulgarly than you think. If, on the other hand, you are aiming at a paper which takes its criticism seriously, I should give you three pieces of serious advice.

"One. Study the works of Aeschylus, Sophocles, Euripides, Shakespeare, Marlowe, Webster, Ford, Beaumont and Fletcher, Molière, Racine, Corneille, Dryden, Wycherley, Congreve, Vanbrugh, Farquhar, Lessing, Schiller, Goldsmith, Sheridan, Ibsen, Strindberg, Sudermann, Hauptmann, Pinero, Wilde, Synge, Galsworthy, O'Neill, O'Casey, Shaw. 'But,' you say, 'I shall be forty before I have mastered these.' To which I reply that you must be at least forty before your opinions can have any value.

"Two. Study the dramatic criticisms of Hazlitt, Lewes, Archer, Shaw, Montague, Walkley, Beerbohm.

"Three. Learn to write English, leave French alone, and avoid quotation unless you are a master of it."

Does this advice fix the standard unnecessarily high? If any young man, holding firm to the determination to become a qualified critic in the theatre, adopted this expert advice, pursued this course of action in order to make sure that eventually criticism that could be justified on sound grounds would result, would he be impelled to realize in the end that academic knowledge had been acquired, that it was largely useless for the fulfilment of practical purposes, and that it

[1] *Ego 5. Again, More of the Autobiography of James Agate.*

could not even be reflected advantageously on the lower but relevant planes of comment in newspapers or periodicals?

Does the critic with a knowledge of the plays of Aeschylus, or Sophocles, or Euripides demonstrate a superiority over his colleague who lacks such knowledge when both are confronted with the necessity to criticize, to appraise, to report on plays by Clemence Dane, Dodie Smith or Esther McCracken or T. S. Eliot, Terence Rattigan or J. B. Priestley? Do Shaw's plays receive stronger, more purposive, more lucid and pertinent appraisal at the hands, and through the brain, of the critic who knows Shakespeare, Marlowe, and Webster through their plays than they receive when dealt with by the intelligent young man who knows little or nothing of the literature of the Elizabethan age to which Shakespeare contributed? Do these names stand for something that is an essential part of the equipment of the highly competent critic in the theatre?

Undoubtedly, the names enumerated in Agate's advice are names of historical significance and of present-day importance. The enumeration furnishes many good debating points, but not necessarily convincing evidence that the young critic in the theatre whose assignment is for 250–500 words on the production of the latest contemporary play will produce more penetrative, more analytical, more purely aesthetical appraisement of play, production, and performance, with special comments on the "stars," if he can pass the Agate test than if he cannot. Westminster Public Libraries

Not clearly defined is the extent to which the critic in the theatre is helped at the beginning of the second half of the twentieth century if he knows, more or less, the place of Sir Arthur W. Pinero in the transitional period that links Restoration drama, petering out under French influence, to an artificial drama of revolt against that influence. This newer drama was, none the less, experimental drama. It laid the foundations of naturalistic drama, which aimed at the incorporation of life in play form and against which, with the poets recurringly attempting to break through into the theatre and to harmonize imagination, inspiration, idealism, the materialistic and the prosaic, reactions set in between the two world wars.

Where does the average theatregoer stand in relation to these movements and vacillations, these doubts and uncertainties, this special knowledge that is acquired to serve practical ends?

The critic in the theatre may, quite legitimately, set for himself a high standard. Does attainment of it help him and also serve, usefully, the primary needs of the average theatregoer?

The historically-minded average theatregoer will see in the performance of a play in the modern theatre something different from, and additional to, what will be seen by the average theatregoer who neither asks for nor expects more than ephemeral entertainment on a superficial plane. Much depends upon the type of play that each supports. Think, illustratively, of *Saint Joan*.

Bernard Shaw made his attitude towards the writing of historical-biographical plays quite clear:[1] "The only way to write a play which shall convey to the general public an impression of antiquity is to make the characters speak blank verse and abstain from reference to steam, telegraphy, or any of the material conditions of their existence. The more ignorant men are, the more convinced are they that their little parish and their little chapel is an apex to which civilization and philosophy has painfully struggled up the pyramid of time from a desert of savagery."

Can the average theatregoer be reasonably expected to relate present and past, to see clearly and in true perspective, whatever that may mean, outstanding personalities who, adopting Henry Arthur Jones's phrase in *Saints and Sinners*, stamped their foot upon their age, and who persist as names but not necessarily as influences? Albert McCleary and Carl Glick, entering a special plea for a contemporary movement in the world of drama, the Community Theatre Movement, touch some of the fringes of the problem in their attempt to bestride drama from its classic beginnings to its relatively unpretentious contemporary expression:[2] "The golden age of Greek Drama, that for all time ennobled tragedy, even though

---

[1] Notes to *Caesar and Cleopatra, Three Plays for Puritans*.
[2] *Curtains Going Up*.

it wailed aloud that mortal man was but the plaything of the gods, contributed the first great corner-stone in the development of the theatre. In England the Elizabethan Period, which gave to the world its greatest literary genius, laid another corner-stone of enduring worth. In between and up to the present day there have been such solitary figures as Terence and Plautus, Racine and Molière, Sheridan and Ibsen, Belasco and the Schuberts, who have done their part. But the history of the theatre has been one of individual, often lonely, figures, each making his contribution. It has been one man against his own age, against his own time, blazing a trail for others to follow. But it is in our own age and time—right now—that the greatest corner-stone of enduring drama has been laid. It hasn't been one man's work alone. It's been the efforts of countless thousands. All of America—the Bill Smiths and Mary Roes of practically every town and city in the United States. They've turned play producers, actors, stage hands, and playwrights—because they loved it. It's been some fifteen million people—one eighth of the nation—the Community Theatre Movement."

This is characteristic American optimism rather than scientifically exact statement. Greek drama, Elizabethan drama, community drama may be "corner-stones," undoubtedly are in the context in which this descriptive label is applied, but wishful thinking elbows out of the way scientific caution when it is suggested that "the greatest corner-stone of enduring drama has been laid." The superlative "greatest" may be accepted for the purpose of progressive evaluation, but the history of drama is, and always will be, incomplete in any civilization that can be prognosticated, and many more pages of it must be written and turned before the appropriateness of the use of "enduring drama" can be admitted.

Time and Values

None the less, there are pertinence and practicality in endeavours that are made to re-value values, to assess the past in terms of the present, to understand the impact of an influence on the people of the generation during which it was virile, and to speculate whether it remains virile as a force or whether it is merely a piece of recorded history with the museum of the recorded past as its most fitting resting place.

Too much importance attached to the past obfuscates the present; concentration on attempts, bound to be futile, to revive the dead prevents the ready recognition of much that is of value in contemporary life. Man cannot for ever master the past before he grapples with the present. Yet his grappling can be facilitated by virile awareness which is dependent upon an appreciation and a placing of that very past in terms of human life which has been lived but which still flows.

Throughout the ages the theatre has made its contribution to life, but it has not been an unchanging contribution. What the theatre meant to the Greeks was not the same, or even closely similar, to what it meant to the people who lived in the Middle Ages. The spirit of the Elizabethan stage was very different from that of its immediate successor, the Restoration age and stage. Robertson, Pinero, and Jones saw what they thought should be their contribution to the theatre, but their theories and aims are seen, in the perspective of the second half of the twentieth century, to have been amateurish and inadequate, theatrically artificial when they were intended to be aggressively actual—but those playwrights themselves could not at the time foresee the stern judgments of those who were to develop and to refine their initial work, although they could quite rightly and without arrogance adjudge themselves to be worthy pioneers, revolutionary adventurers engaged in the advancement of what was considered to be a worthy cause.

Ashley Dukes has an illuminating comment on this aspect of the link between stage and spectator. It may be, he states,[1] "poetic and ecstatic, as it was in the Greek theatre; or religious and boisterous, as in the theatre of the Middle Ages; or popular and imaginative, as in the theatre of the Elizabethans; or aristocratic and fashionable, as in the theatre of the Restoration; or sentimental and melodramatic, as in the theatre of the nineteenth century; or social and critical, as in the theatre of our own day. But the link is always established; and in so far as drama mirrors life, it mirrors the spiritual feeling of its audience. We must therefore think of the audience not only

[1] *Drama.*

as a passive witness of the dramatic spectacle, but as an active and creative participant. Periods of greatness in dramatic art have always reflected an awakening of social consciousness, like that of the Athenian civilization at its height and of the stirring and adventurous age of the Renaissance. In the same way, periods of littleness have always reflected an indifference to the theatre and a withdrawal of cultivated minds to other forms of expression. A drama that is despised (as it was despised by some of the best writers of the nineteenth century, for example) can produce no masterpiece. A drama that is respected and fostered by general interest gives of its noblest in return."

These considerations bring to the surface some of the undercurrents of thought and feeling, and serve to give pleasurable definition to the lines of demarcation that divide one section of the theatre-loving community from another.

I draw upon personal experience for illustrative matter.

When years ago I was a citizen in a West Country city, Bath, with its great theatrical traditions, I was associated with two organizations, the first, a playgoers' society; the second, a modern drama club. The membership of both split— "naturally" is, I think, the operative adverb—into two sections. The members of one section emphasized, in my opinion unwisely, the importance of organizing through recreative activities a knowledge of the plays of "the moderns," with Bernard Shaw a prominent favourite, and were antagonistic to the taking of even occasional glances backward at the plays of the Restoration and Elizabethan ages "because they were dated and had nothing of supreme value to say to men and women destined by the accident of time and circumstance to wrestle with contemporary problems." On the other hand, members of the opposing section had a spontaneous liking for the plays of these two ages, and could find nothing objectionable in the indulgences of the Restorationists in licence rather than liberty, but could bristle with moral indignation at the pointed seriousness of the moderns who wrote about prostitution and its economic returns (*Mrs. Warren's Profession*), about venereal disease and its effects (*Ghosts* and *Damaged Goods*), public life and immorality (*Waste*).

The members of both sections tended to have closed minds. They could see little that was good in any side other than their own, and had little, if any, inclination to weigh and consider opposing points of view, whether they were expressed by superficial enthusiasts or by deep-knowledged professors and experts. The reminder that there is something to be entered on both sides of any profit and loss account; that no body of doctrine, no set of first principles of any party or sect, is beyond comment, criticism, and appraisement, is platitudinous—and also apposite.

Bernard Shaw included in his Maxims for Revolutionaries what is a helpful, working axiom for critics, *The Golden Rule Is That There Is No Rule.*

Similarly, the critic does well to remember that there is something to be said for the avoidance of heroes. If, however, hero-worshipping becomes an integral part of an individual's sincere appreciation, then an effective brake on the development of the spirit of crass and stupid idolatry is, intermittently, to take the hero (or heroine) from his pedestal to give him a good intellectual dusting.

My associates in the West Country had several heroes.

A professor and his wife thought Euripides was incomparable. Now Euripides is rightly described by the use of superlatives, but to insist that he must be kept out of reach of comparison is to brush aside the validity of sound, disinterested criticism.

Shakespeare was another hero of another couple, husband and wife, whose professional interests had, for years, kept Shakespeare alive in their lives without creating the revulsion or causing the uncomplimentary reactions that are sometimes sequential to an imposed obligation to become expert in the analysis, interpretation, and expression of the works of any master-mind.

Whatever Shakespeare is, or was, he could, figuratively, be endowed by them with Godhead only. There is a great deal to be said about him, and for him, which pays just tribute to the uniqueness of his stature as a genius whose works embody many facets of greatness in expression, but there is also something that is relevant that can be said to demonstrate that even

a genius is not the personification of Perfection, and also to
serve as a reminder of one fact that the critic ignores or forgets
only to lower his own critical standard: in the march of
time not only are the pages of the calendar turned, but
also, inevitably, changes in tastes, in ideas, in evaluations
are born.

William Archer had these, or similar, points in mind, either
consciously or subconsciously, when he, in no mischievous
spirit, wrote critically about Shakespeare and his contemporaries:[1] "The disappearance in modern drama of the hard-
and-fast line of demarcation between tragedy and comedy has
often been noted, and sometimes set down as a symptom of
degeneration. It marks, in fact, the completion of an age-long
process, and the final release of drama from the fetters imposed
upon it by a tradition which had its origins in prehistoric
tribal life.

"Here, then, we have, I think, some approach to a rational
principle of appreciation: we can recognize as good, as in
harmony with an inevitable tendency, any abandonment of
exaggerative, in favour of soberly imitative, methods. We see
that in rejecting the rent and rhetoric of conventional tragedy,
the habitual over-emphasis, often passing into buffoonery, of
conventional comedy, we have not been falling away from a
state of aesthetic grace, but purifying the art of drama from
extrinsic elements. We recognize the emptiness of the oft-
repeated complaint that we neglect on the modern stage the
marvellous treasures of our classical drama, from, I suppose,
Marlowe to Sheridan Knowles. The truth is that a just instinct
has told us that the great mass of Elizabethan, Restoration
and eighteenth-century plays have nothing to say to modern
audiences, because they exemplify primitive and transitional
types of art, portray, with much exaggeration, gross and
unpleasing manners, and call for forms of virtuosity in repre-
sentation which are well-nigh extinct on the modern stage.
The towering genius of Shakespeare overcame the imperfec-
tions of the form in which he worked, and gave to the stage of
the whole world a series of ever-living masterpieces; but even
in regard to Shakespeare it is folly to deny that a good many

[1] *The Old Drama and The New.*

of his minor works, and a good many passages in his major works, belong to his age and not to all time. That is not to say that I am opposed to revivals of his minor works, and even of certain plays of his contemporaries and immediate successors. There is room on a well-organized stage for educational and antiquarian performances. What I do say is that the people who extol the semi-barbarous drama of the minor Elizabethans as something vastly superior to the drama of today have no conception of the true essence of drama, and found their opinion (in so far as it has any rational foundation at all) on a palpable confusion between drama and lyric poetry. They deplore as an unmixed disaster that sloughing-off of the extrinsic elements of passion and exaggeration which I, on the contrary, represent to you as not only an inevitable, but in the main an extremely desirable, process."

Prejudices and Judgments

This quotation my West Country associates who were Shakespearean fanatics—the husband and wife were not alone in their unqualified admiration—rejected as an example of an acknowledged expert's perverse debunking. So strong was the prejudice that keen appreciation evoked, that any attempts to discuss the subject judicially were instantly quashed. There could be no discussion on a subject that had been dealt with conclusively for all time! The critical faculty was deliberately jerked out of gear; the mental machinery, in running order, was permitted to run on, but on this question, at any rate, dynamic driving force was not generated. The non-critical contenders of the unquestioned superiority of Greek drama, or of Elizabethan drama, or of Restoration drama, were not, however, alone.

The moderns were equally as lop-sided in their views and evaluations. With some of them Bernard Shaw was the modern god. Had he not given expression to iconoclastic opinions that his contemporaries and predecessors had lacked the courage—or the inclination—to bring into the arena of public discussion? Were not his plays rich in idea-content? Was not his advocacy, in play form, of revolutionary reforms considered, strong, and severe? They battened, as the others had, on aspects of truth, but they had not in their grasp the truth, the whole truth, and nothing but the truth.

Tradition, purity of form, sound characterization, art and propaganda, the poet in the theatre, the legitimacy of mixing opposites, i.e. grave and gay, the superficial and the fundamental, wit, wisecrack, and mere wordage, the repression of human emotions and the over-valuation of the intellect—here are some aspects of thought that have relevance to the subject-matter that can usefully be surveyed when attempts are made to assess comparative values. These are of primary importance to the critic in the theatre, although there may be some commentators who would affirm that dramatic values are but slightly related to dramatic criticism. To any such the suggestion is made that drama in its challenging shadows and subtleties, its conflicts and its cohesions, is the indispensable material that is passed through the theatre. It must, therefore, be comprehended by the critic in the theatre, for he cannot function soundly while remaining ignorant of its inherent texture, which is rightly evaluated only when ability to compare is both possessed and applied.

The literature of drama contains an inexhaustible supply of interesting points for useful discussion. It is worth studying: it should be studied by the young man (or young woman) who is more than slightly concerned with the sound development of drama and the theatre, and who wishes to acquire special knowledge more comprehensive than that which constitutes the equipment of the average theatregoer. On occasions, it will not be possible to come to a definite conclusion. There cannot be exactitude of measurement. Whether Shakespeare was greater than Shaw, or better than Shaw; whether Shaw had more to say to the modern world than Shakespeare ever said to the people who were alive and also heard his words spoken in the Globe Theatre in the sixteenth century; whether the blank verse of Shakespeare, more suited to his own day than straightforward prose would have been, is superior or inferior to Shaw's lucid, concise, rhythmic, direct, rhetorical prose in which his prefaces and plays were written—all these can be, and often are, the starting-points of discussions that generate more heat than even horse sense, but they are not necessarily futile.

They can serve as scavengers and get rid of some of the undesirable refuse that clogs intellectual analyses. For example, did Shaw ever seriously contend that his plays are better than Shakespeare's plays?

I have heard Shakespeare enthusiasts, engaged in disputation, declare emphatically that he did, their declarations being uttered with astringent contempt that was intended to dismiss Shaw as a bumptious humbug for having given utterance to such a heresy and to bring discussion to a sharp close.

I have also heard Shaw enthusiasts, similarly engaged, aver that they do not care whether Shaw had or had not claimed to be Shakespeare's superior. In their opinion he was, and as far as they were concerned that was their verdict—and it was conclusive! This example can appropriately be rounded off by giving the origin of this recurring, contentious point:[1] "It will be said that these remarks" (this is given in the section that is entitled "Better Than Shakespear") "can bear no other construction than an offer of my Caesar to the public as an improvement on Shakespear's. And in fact, that is their precise purport. But here let me give a friendly warning to those scribes who have so often exclaimed against my criticisms of Shakespear as blasphemous against a hitherto unquestioned Perfection and Infallibility. Such criticisms are no more new than the creed of my Diabolonian Puritan or my revival of the humors of Cool as a Cucumber. Too much surprise at them betrays an acquaintance with Shakespear criticism so limited as not to include even the prefaces of Dr. Johnson and the utterances of Napoleon. I have merely repeated in the dialect of my own time and in the light of its philosophy what they said in the dialect and light of theirs. Do not be misled by the Shakespear fanciers who, ever since his own time, have delighted in his plays just as they might have delighted in a particular breed of pigeons if they had never learnt to read. His genuine critics, from Ben Jonson to Mr. Frank Harris, have always kept as far on this side idolatry as I."

There is genuine value in drawing upon sources and origins. They constitute some of the essential bases of comparison upon

[1] Preface to *Three Plays for Puritans*.

which the critic in the theatre builds. He cannot afford to be insular. To be aware of the evolution of drama in English literature will not suffice, although it will be of practical value. Influences and forces that have been generated by the dramatists of countries which, on first thoughts, may seem to have little or no connexion with what has developed in Britain, explain, in part, why British drama began to develop in a certain way at a point in its history that can be clearly marked.

I am aware that this attitude of mind can be disadvantageously stressed, that the links that bind past, present, and future have little, if any, relevance to immediate practicalities; that they can, so to speak, be seen only through the eyes of the expert whose primary concern may be with the history of the ages rather than with the record of the immediate moment.

C. H. Norman, in *The Revolutionary Spirit in Modern Literature and Drama and The Class War of Europe* 1918–36 stated that "men of genius, working through the dramatic medium, throw open the dark places of the world to the inspection of all who are affected by them in their lives. The historian details, and sometimes denounces, the errors of the dead; the dramatist demands the attention of the living for their purification and for the social advantage."

Censorship of Plays

This quotation raises, indirectly, interesting queries. I will cite one emergent point. The critic in the theatre who serves his profession for years in modern society will probably, on some occasion, be confronted with the necessity to declare himself for or against the censorship of plays—or, perhaps, of one particular play. Will he be helped in his attempts to form sound judgment if he knows—I ought, maybe, to say because he knows—the origin of censorship in the theatre? The plays that have been censored—for a time—have, later, been acknowledged as important contributions to drama: *Ghosts, Damaged Goods, Mrs. Warren's Profession, Waste, Monna Vanna, The Breaking Point,* etc. Other plays have been censored. Is there any connexion between the censorship of plays and Mr. Norman's contention that "the dramatist demands the attention of the living for their purification and for the social

advantage"? Are contemporary politicians quite immune
from influences that were operative when Walpole's corrupt
administration led to the introduction of censorship to safeguard the privileges and abuses of erring and straying
politicians?

The censorship of stage plays has been the subject of official
inquiry on several occasions. There is still a problem of
censorship. Years ago I asked Bernard Shaw to write for me
and for publication an article on the censorship of stage plays.
He replied, in effect, that he had solved the problem years ago,
and that he was unwilling at his advanced age to re-cover the
ground—unnecessarily from his point of view. Why is it that
some of the plays that have been censored as being unfit for
public performance have, with the passing of time, been
licensed as suitable plays for public presentation? Are the
decisions rooted in principle or in expediency? Ibsen's
Ghosts is a challenging example. When this play was first
produced at the Royalty in 1891 the critics spoke, with voices
that were almost unanimous, in condemnation of the playwright, the play, the players, and the playgoers. Its history is
well worth tracing by students of drama and the theatre, and
especially by those who are in search of material on which to
form an opinion on the working of the censorship of stage plays.

The critic's bases of comparison can be taken from another
angle.

After the economic and political revolutions in Russia,
which, in essence, began the process of splitting the world into
two camps, the politicians, recognizing the value of theatre and
stage, used drama purposively for education as well as entertainment. The creative literary artists, the imaginative word-
spinners, the idealistic theorists who could theorize through
the medium of the written word, the adaptable users of
language for the attainment of clearly-conceived and well-
defined ends, tied expression to intention and made dramatic
and theatrical art subservient to political ambitions and aims.
In short, they raised once again the issue of the permissibility
of fusing dramatic art and political propaganda. In the
interpretation of the legitimacy of their work and its effectiveness, was there anything of value to be extracted from the

underlying intentions of those who laid the foundation-stones of English drama?

Truth Is Relative

What were the intentions of the writers of the moralities, miracles, and interludes, and of subsequent writers who influenced the development of English drama? What were the purposes for which they were used by those who were in a position to impose them on the common people? Was early drama religious and didactic alike? Was "pure" entertainment of the illiterate people the sole aim? Did the "leaders" see in drama an educational instrument that could be wielded entertainingly? A common presupposition is that those who are actively engaged on the performance of a task know precisely what they are doing and why they are doing it. It is assumed that their activities spring from the conviction that they have grasped "truth absolute." But, in final analysis, truth is relative.

Propaganda in drama can be deliberate distortion, but, in retrospect, are the writers of the religious plays of the Middle Ages accepted as infallible? Even if the premiss that they wrote to express a deep religious spirit be accepted, can we, with equal readiness of acceptance, proclaim that the facts were not distorted? In this context distortion needs to be related to time, place, and circumstance. Were not the writers of propaganda plays writing to express a deep political spirit? Some of them were, undoubtedly, opportunists, but this particular breed of facile propagandists is not of one epoch only.

Think of the dramatists in Russia who were writing immediately after the twin revolutions (political and economic) which began to shape, and are still shaping, the direction of world development. Let there be recognition—niggardly, if in accordance with mood—that a significant, small minority may have been sincerely in harmony with the aims and trends of the revolutionary politicians—what then? Were they in spiritual integrity, intellectual calibre, moral weight, ethical judgment, disconcertingly below the standard that characterizes those writers in the Middle Ages who wrote to express "a deep religious spirit?" A 1952 report on the Russian theatre stated that "more than 200 plays are showing in the Moscow playhouses," and struck the jubilant note that "every night the theatres of the capital, which are open to the entire people, are crowded out."

It is true that there is a basic difference between "religious spirit" and "political spirit," but when attempts are made, after acceptance of this fact, to understand and to interpret it, what follows? That in the Middle Ages there was, as a concomitant of religious fervour and complacent orthodoxy, persecution of the irreligious, and that in modern times there is, as a concomitant of political sincerity and rationalized orthodoxy, persecution of the politically unorthodox but, nevertheless, politically rationalized?

The Russians were not the only nationals at whom the politicians aimed with political propaganda clothed as dramatic and theatre art.

When, in 1938, I toured Germany I saw, on several occasions, a number of audiences of tens of thousands of open-air theatre-goers whose emotions more than their minds, perhaps, were being worked upon by the manufacturers of theatrical entertainment—in some cases creative dramatists would be an untenable appellation. The underlying intention was to mould opinions and functioning in such ways as to make them harmonize with the then German way of life.

Again, can anything be gained by the critic in the theatre who, thinking historically, recognizes and relates the purposes for which drama has been used as an instrument throughout the ages? Admittedly, it seems to be a far cry from, say, the Aldwych farces of Ben Travers to the farcical or comedic interludes that are components of some of Shakespeare's plays. But just as the groundlings had to be served in the days of the Elizabethans, so Mr. John Citizen, The Common Man, or whatever may be the current designation, must be deliberately, though subconsciously to some degree, moulded to the way of life as it is lived in his stratum of modern society, with its existing phases of organization.

The same subject can be approached from an entirely different angle.

W. Somerset Maugham, in his first volume of autobiography, *The Summing Up*, became a prophet about the development of drama. One thing seems certain, he contends—that if the stage play has any chance at all of survival, it is not by trying to do any longer what the pictures can do better, adding that possibly the dramatist would be wise now to go back to the origins of modern drama and call to his aid verse, dancing, music, and pageantry so that he might appeal to all possible sources of entertainment, and hazarding that, perhaps, the best chance the realistic dramatist has today is to occupy himself with what, till now at all events, the screen has not succeeded very well in presenting—the drama in which the action is inner rather than outer and the comedy of wit.

If we accept Maugham's prophetic vision as realism for the purpose of conducting a personal inquiry into the likelihood of change in modern drama, and if we also accept the suggestion that the poet must return to the theatre, do we reach the conclusion that through, say, T. S. Eliot or Christopher Fry, the theologian may also return, via instructive drama "in which the action is inner rather than outer," to the theatre? Alternatively, if we think that the accent of the future must be on some expression or reflection of collectivism, do we assume, rightly or wrongly, that a writer of the type of, say, Clifford Odets or even J. B. Priestley in some of his moods, may be the herald of a new type of dramatist who will re-introduce into the theatre the propagandist-playwright?

There is not, I submit, any one, final irrevocable answer to these and other relevant questions that can be asked.

My intention in this chapter has been to focus attention on the potentialities and possibilities of diversified approach to the study of drama and to the appraisement of plays of any type that are passed through the modern theatre for the entertainment of the theatregoing public—and also to gratify the profit desires of the promoters. I do not think that the present-day critic in the theatre *must* know all that Agate stated he should know. On the other hand, I do not deny that the knowledge posited by Agate in his advice is capable of being turned to aesthetic as well as practical ends. The mainspring of the critic's functioning must be an integral part of his machinery. What it is, or should be, and what ends it serves, depend upon many factors. Some are inescapably materialistic; some are of the non-practical world and as such have little, if anything, to do with occupational activities or money-making necessities.

CHAPTER III

THE CRITIC'S TASTES AND VALUES

THE theatregoer goes to the theatre for a variety of reasons, any one of which has a bearing on the natural desire of human beings to be entertained. The author who writes plays probably also acts in response to varied motives. Expression in play form may be his best medium. He may be desirous of the quick financial returns that arise out of a commercial success in the theatre. He may have in mind the even more impressive monetary rewards of a screen success that is based on a successful production of a play in the West End, followed by the additional benefits that accrue from performances by repertory companies, touring companies, at home or abroad, amateur societies, and play readings. He may have strong opinions on the platform-pulpit possibilities of the stage. He may be ambitious for social recognition and see in theatrical publicity a short cut to the realization of ambition. He may be a creative literary artist in doubt, and be able to resolve the doubt only after serious and prolonged reflection. Charles Morgan's *The River Line* was written in the form of a novel two years or so before it was produced and performed at the 1952 Edinburgh Festival in play form. *Why* is brought out in its printed version by the playwright-novelist-essayist's explanation of his attitude towards subject, theme, and treatment.

The business man in the theatre thinks of plays in terms of saleable commodities, is unlikely rather than likely to be specially interested in aesthetic, cultural, or other qualities that have not a direct bearing on speculative capital investment for profit, and endeavours, as the writer of would-be commercially successful plays must endeavour, first to assess public taste for theatrical entertainment, and then to satisfy it.

The critic goes to the theatre in his capacity of critic because he must. His duty is to be aware of public taste and of how those who are interested in it cater for it, and also to assess relative values. What he writes may be sound interpretation and evaluation. If it is favourable, he may be instrumental in influencing public demand to see the play that he has appraised; if it is unfavourable, he may be one of a number of destructive forces that make commercial success short-lived or impracticable.

There are other influences, either progressive or reactionary, at work in the world of the theatre. Some impinge upon art and its expression; some upon commerce and its activities. The certainty is that through the ordinary commercial theatre, the experimental theatre, the repertory theatre, the fashionable theatre in the heart of London's West End, or the unassuming, in some cases almost apologetic, provincial theatre are passed varied types of theatrical entertainment—comedy, farce, melodrama, burlesque, revue; plays in verse; plays with music; manufactured concoctions that make their strongest direct appeal to the eye; similar manufactures that stimulate the primitive in man.

The average theatregoer is often unaware of the subtle differences in the richly varied theatrical entertainment with which he is provided, although it is probable that he will be able to state his preferences, even though he may be unable to rationalize them.

The commercial man of the theatre trades in certainties rather than gambles speculatively when he decides to invest in the provision of light popular theatrical entertainment. He knows that there are more theatregoers who prefer to be "amused" than "instructed" in the theatre, but even the experienced business man cannot be certain in advance that what he considers is material for the profitable amusement of theatregoers will, in result, bring him the schemed-for financial returns.

The playwright whose written expression springs from his desire to make money quickly, and who writes in accordance with rationalized anticipation of success when he writes to a formula that he has convinced himself is the one that must be followed to enable him to attain his ends, often finds that he has miscalculated and misjudged public taste, and is disappointed. Disappointment is often the result when he has written imaginatively and with the foreknowledge of a success already achieved by what he considers to be similar writing in a similar vein.

This inability to calculate, and to judge soundly in advance of testing, both public taste and public demand for theatrical entertainment is the explanation of why one "thriller" may be an instantaneous theatrical success and another similar one a failure that is seen to be what it is on the first night of its performance. Public taste exists, but is elusive and chameleon-like in its capacity for change. It is there to be catered for, with success, but it is often capricious, satiated with a quickness that confounds—hence "flops" in all types of theatrical entertainment.

Even imaginative, careful, and flawless writing to a tried and proved formula will not necessarily yield the type of entertainment that will amuse the average theatregoer. More than half a century ago Henry Arthur Jones, who during his playwriting career had a measure of success in writing plays that he calculated would make money to enable him to live on his earnings and also to write plays that would satisfy his aesthetic self, lectured to a Bradford audience, taking for his title "On Being Rightly Amused at the Theatre." It was suggested by a passage from the French critic Sainte-Beuve quoted by the English critic Matthew Arnold: "In France the first consideration is not whether we are amused and pleased by a work of art or mind, nor is it whether we are touched by it. What we seek above all to learn is whether we are *right* in being amused with it, and in applauding in it, and in being moved by it." Jones, developing his theme, said:[1] ". . . to avoid ambiguity we will put the maxim thus: 'The *first* end of a play is to amuse: the *chief* end of a play is to amuse rightly.' But you reply, 'If we *are* amused, if we go to the theatre and have a good laugh or a good cry, and enjoy ourselves, what do we want to bother any further about it? What's the use of asking ourselves whether we were right or wrong? What does it matter?' If you were enjoying a certain course of living, and your doctor told you that it would gradually undermine your health, don't you think it would matter whether you continued it or not? And it does matter, and it has a permanent influence upon

[1] *The Renascence of the English Drama.*

your character and intellectual health, whether you laugh at
this jest or that, whether you harden and wither your heart
with witless drivel and imbecility, or whether you bathe and
ease and enlarge it at such fountains of wise merriment as
Sheridan and Goldsmith, Fielding and Dickens, Cervantes
and Rabelais. But I am sure that a representative body of
playgoers . . . will readily assent when I say that there is a
right way and a wrong way of being amused, and that it is
of considerable importance, both to the drama itself as an
intellectual art, and to the character of its patrons, that
they should know when they are being rightly amused at the
theatre."

Who must be the arbiter on this important question of the
provision of theatrical entertainment that the providers hope
and expect will amuse? Who is the one who will guess correctly
and in advance the theatregoers' reactions to it, reactions
which, on occasions, produce boredom, not amusement;
irritation, not satisfaction; embarrassment, not acquiescence?
Obviously, the commercial men who operate in the theatre,
notwithstanding their speculative propensities, have convinced
themselves that what they intend "to present" will amuse
those to whom they make their appeal through poster and
advertisement. They have in mind theatregoers whose
numerical strength is such that profit accrues from what they
pay to be amused. But the commercial men may be wrong, in
which case they pay for their wrongness.

Amusement in the Theatre

The average theatregoer, by his theatregoing, places
himself in a position to state whether he has been "rightly
amused" by what he has seen and heard. If he is able to deliver
a favourable verdict, the fact that he has been amused will be
confirmation of the soundness of the organization of theatrical
entertainment by the business man in the theatre. But should
the average theatregoer be amused? Again, it must be asked:
"Who must decide?" "The *first* end of a play is to amuse,"
Jones said. This is a dogmatic statement that can be defended
successfully only if one can accept facets of the Absolute, and
be unassailably satisfied that amusement is, indeed, the first

end of any play of any type, and that amusement has been defined beyond doubt. A similar remark applies to the rightness of the amusement, which, said Jones, must be the *chief* (another categorical word that is open to question) end of a play. A safe assumption is that thousands of theatregoers have been amused by a light comedy, say a Coward or an Esther McCracken comedy, and rightly amused. Equally applicable is the statement that thousands of theatregoers have been amused by a play of serious ideas, say, one of Shaw's polemical but witty flashes of brilliance, or of St. John Ervine's virile treatment of contemporary issues.

A problem of individual taste is involved, and the cultivation of this, in whatever state it happens to be at a specific moment, has not necessarily anything to do with training that has for object the attainment of what the authorities, the specialists, the guides, philosophers, and friends of the average theatregoer aver to be desirable—even essential—intellectual, aesthetic, and cultural standards without which life cannot be enjoyed to the full.

Individual taste is affected, developed, vitiated, refined by objective personal forces and the impact of impersonal influences that are inescapable, as well as by the deliberate rationalization of personal interests and activities that have unwavering subjective approval.

The average theatregoer, exercising freedom of choice, is a haphazard seeker after theatrical entertainment. He enters the theatre hopefully, and leaves it, after two hours or so inside, pleased or displeased, disappointed or satisfied, with individual appraisal that he has had value for his money or that his expenditure has not been rewarded adequately. In short, he knows what his own consciousness tells him about what he has seen and heard in the theatre, and it is unlikely that he is capable of being converted instantaneously to any other evaluation, though to admit this is not to deny the possible effects of a policy of effective permeation. If his preference is for comedy, and he is prejudiced against tragedy, he will, indulging his theatregoing habits, choose to see a play that he thinks, in advance, will amuse him, and he will not be concerned whether amusement is the first end of that particular play or, subsequently, whether, assuming that he has been amused, his amusement was legitimate.

This attitude towards theatregoing of the average theatregoer acknowledges the status of the individual and his importance as an individual. Acknowledgment can be too generous, but it is unlikely to go farther astray than is dogmatic theorizing about what ought and ought not to be rightly amusing to the average theatregoer. The entertainment-seeker who finds what he wants in comedy will remain, for a time at any rate, unmoved by analyses, however sound, of the qualities, superior or distinctive, of tragedy, and it is not glaringly obvious why a policy of conversion should be launched against him by those whose taste is for tragedy, although there is much to be said for or against an excluding narrowness or a non-discriminating acceptance on broad foundations. L. A. G. Strong is helpfully balanced in his consideration of the appeal of tragedy when he writes:[1] "There is in the mind of the average theatregoer a prejudice against tragedy. 'When I go to the theatre I want to see something cheerful. There is enough pain and tragedy in ordinary life, without showing it to us on the stage.' If he does not use this well-tried formula, he will complain of a tragic play that it is 'morbid' and 'depressing.' So some plays are, without doubt; but such plays fail to be tragic. There is nothing morbid or depressing about tragedy. The Greeks, who were accustomed to sit out trilogies of three tragedies on end, valued them for their cathartic or purifying effect upon the emotions. The tragedies of Shakespeare draw audiences again and again. *Hamlet* in particular can be relied upon to fill a theatre. It is not only that the story is exciting, that it offers opportunities for great acting, that it contains passages familiar to the majority of educated people. It is that, again and again, it engages their sympathies, stirs their emotions, and fortifies them in their struggle with circumstance. No play in our language comprehends so wide a range of life. It appeals to the navvy in the gallery as well as to the connoisseur in the stalls. It has something for everybody. Naturally, no one is always in the mood for tragedy. There are times when we need to laugh, when we deliberately avoid anything which will

[1] *Common Sense About Drama.*

challenge our mind or our emotions. But if we restrict our theatregoing to these occasions, we are going to miss one of the greatest sources of strength and pleasure which life has to offer. It is difficult, in England, at any rate, not to sound priggish when talking of the pleasure one gets from art. When the man who frequents symphony concerts assures one that he also loves jazz, we are apt to imagine in his voice a note of condescension. However, the risk must be run."

Mr. Strong wrote with the average theatregoer in mind. He (or she) is the victim, fortunate or unfortunate, of the state of society into which he is born and in which he develops. It will not be altogether his fault if his taste is latent or undeveloped, for what he is capable of appreciating and appraising is far different from what he chooses to see as entertainment for his pleasure.

Theatregoing remains an expression of individual taste and requirements. It creates fashion and it follows fashion. Sometimes it is the fashion to see a so-called highbrow play; sometimes the correct thing is to see a grimly naturalistic play. More often public enthusiasm is for a delightful comedy. Sometimes a prevailing taste for a romantic costume play, or for a successful "thriller," dictates theatregoing habits. On balance, "light" entertainment makes the strongest appeal to theatregoers who wish to be amused, and they are not fastidious about the rightness of the amusement. This submission to the relatively undisturbing play, the play that offers avenues of escape from reality while seemingly introducing into the theatre the brighter, the lighter, sides of life that is lived romantically, superficially, artificially, rather than with a grim naturalism that is accompanied by strenuous attempts to wrestle with life's problems—an inescapable wrestling by some in any modern civilization—can reasonably be expected to persist.

When, in its origins, drama was educative, the educational appeal was appetizingly coated. "Comedy . . . developed before tragedy, in the history of the English drama. When the drama, which had been fostered by the Church," points out A. S. Rapport,[1] "had emancipated itself from ecclesiastic

[1] *The English Drama.*

control, had passed into the hands of the people and become an element of their amusements, comedy naturally took the foremost rank. It appeals to the people, to the general audience, who wished to laugh and to be amused, much more readily than tragedy. Comedy also stands nearer to reality, for it can find its subjects anywhere by simply copying real life. 'Comedy,' says Mr. Symonds, 'attracts an uninstructed audience more powerfully than Tragedy. Of this we have plenty of evidence in our own days, when the "better vulgar" crowd the Music Hall, and gather to Burlesque, but barely lounge at fashion's beck to a Shakespearean Revival. Comedy of the average type can be more easily invented than Tragedy. It appeals to a commoner intelligence. It deals with more familiar motives. Lastly, but by no means least, it makes far slighter demands upon the capacity of actors. Passing over into caricature, it is not only tolerable, but oftentimes enhanced in effect. Whereas Tragedy, hyperbolised—Herod out-Heroding Herod—becomes supremely ridiculous.' It is for these reasons that Comedy preceded Tragedy on the English Stage. It must also be borne in mind that Tragedy is more in need of models, and requires a study of classic antiquity. It is therefore in Tragedy that foreign influence made itself felt, exercising its power upon the early development of the regular English Drama. This influence dates from the Italian Renaissance and the Revival of Learning."

A Nation's Theatres

This comparison of comedy and tragedy can usefully be pondered in conjunction with one of St. John Ervine's characteristic assertions:[1] "When a nation is weakest, physically and spiritually, its people will not listen to tragedy, but demand what is called light entertainment: comic plays, spectacular pieces, trivial shows. Of the four great Greek dramatists who have survived to us, three—Aeschylus, Sophocles and Euripides, were tragedians, and one, Aristophanes, was a comedian. The Elizabethans preferred to write tragedies rather than comedies, and seemingly they had no trouble in getting audiences for them. Shakespeare wrote every kind of play,

[1] *The Organized Theatre.*

from farce to tragedy, but is remembered by us more for his tragedies than for his comedies. . . . And what is true of him is largely true of his contemporaries. Here, surely, is a paradox. When Greece was greatest, the tragic dramatists were predominant. In the great age of England, when there was less individual poverty than there is now, when the people were happy and adventurous and fortunate and full of courage, the dramatists were predominantly engaged in writing tragedies. How are we to account for this singular fact? . . . one can hardly deny that when a nation's theatres are mainly, and even exclusively, occupied by trivial and comic and spectacular pieces, that nation is either in deep distress or its mind is bankrupt. There is something demented about a man who is continually giggling. It is not natural to healthy, normal-minded people always to be roaring with laughter."

Does it follow, automatically, that the members of a nation that has been made strong, both physically and spiritually, will, in consequence, delight most in tragedy?

The Germany of the 1930's was strong physically—and spiritually, if things of the spirit spring from the assimilation and expression of religious fervour—according to the views of some people, but there was no obvious turning to tragedy of the hero-worshippers of the Hitler régime. Rather were they "soaked" in romantic history and colourful pageantry. Nor can it be said that the Russians of the post-economic and political revolutions turned naturally to tragedy. They were inclined, possibly aided by propagandist methods, to "plays with a purpose," to the symbolic and expressionistic, to drama of social significance, which, playing upon the emotions through unusual presentation of ideas in play form, struck an optimistic note in picturesque attractiveness in order to induce the people, grown enthusiastic, to work for the attainment of materialistic ends, without, however, wholly ignoring the place of the intellect and the spiritual in individual or communal life. Nevertheless, leaving the Greeks and the Elizabethans out of detailed consideration, overlooking the licence and the excesses of the Restorationists, and thinking of the moderns, something can be said in support of Mr. Ervine's contentions.

Even the average theatregoer does not always get what he

wants. What is provided for him is an estimate of what he wishes to see, and when he sees it pleasurable expectations may not be realized, although they are not based on aesthetic and intellectual demands. When the average theatregoer enters the theatre, if he is there to see the presentation of a naturalistic play, a performance of Galsworthy's *The Skin Game* or of St. John Ervine's *Robert's Wife*, naturalistic tests can be applied. Are the characters "true to life?" By this is meant "Does the playwright make his characters speak and act so that they convey the impression that they are functioning in real life?" "Is there plausibility in what they say and do?" Mr. Ervine himself, in his "Present Time Appraisal"[1] of another dramatist, Oscar Wilde, which is a highly individualized and keenly provocative study that excites curiosity, commands agreement, and arouses disagreement, makes numerous pertinent points, two of which, I recall, are (i) a dramatist who sets out to reveal life should reveal life and not fanciful fiction; and (ii) it is his business to know his characters so well that he can answer any questions about them.

There will be differences of opinion. The critic in the theatre, if not the average theatregoer, understands the selective processes that were at work when the creative artist was engaged in his act of creation. The sound critic does not have his prejudices readily aroused. His emotions do not get out of control. He sees any type of entertainment in historical perspective, which brings a generous measure of agreement with A. R. Skemp, when he wrote: "All art reveals the vision of the world and of life seen through a temperament. The greatest artists disguise nothing and distort nothing; but seeing wide as well as deep, they find balance and harmony in the whole. They see ugliness and beauty, sorrow and joy, cruelty and pity, terror and triumphant faith, weakness and strength— not isolated, but blended in infinite variety; and the greatest artists thus preserve, in the revelation of each aspect of life, the truth of a wider vision. So Homer and Euripides, Dante and Chaucer, Shakespeare and Molière, Goethe, and Browning, Fielding, Balzac and Meredith. It is not a question of optimism or pessimism, or even of the selection of comic or pathetic or

[1] *Oscar Wilde.*

tragic material. It is a question of width of outlook and health of vision."

Types of entertainment are readily recognizable by the average theatregoer, who may not, however, be able to differentiate them in terms of language.

It is the function of the critic in the theatre to make clear basic differences and the results that get themselves reflected in the playwright's work when he keeps clearly in mind the significance of differences.

The average theatregoer, it is accepted, goes to the theatre to be amused. Whether he is amused or not, and what the level of his amusement is, are conditioned by circumstances. In some theatres on some occasions occupants of the stalls and the dress circle are spontaneous in their applause, which, however, is accompanied by "boos" that originate in the gallery and the pit.

The critic goes to the theatre, I reiterate, to engage in evaluation. He is not there to please himself, but to interpret how and why the average theatregoer, multiplied until he becomes the audience in the theatre, reacts to the performance on the stage. His own taste must be kept in subjection. As an individual, what he has to assess may represent for him boredom unmitigated. As a critic he has to see theatrical entertainment in perspective and through the minds of hundreds of theatre-goers each of whom is unique. He must be the Dr. Jekyll and Mr. Hyde of criticism. He has to play a part. His playing of it is helped when he knows not only what it is, but also from what it has evolved, although his concise criticism may give him no scope whatever for stating the grounds on which his evaluations are based. If he is a mature critic, one who is able to draw upon long and varied experience, he is able to contrast, say, the craze for "musicals" from America with the different but not necessarily better, musical comedies of the old Gaiety days. His own taste in music may be for melody, for smooth progression, for "a tune that titillates the ear."

He may regret keenly that the types of entertainment that appealed to him during the days of his youth are no longer provided, but in assessing what is provided he tries to compare in order to reach his conclusions on values. His own values he may find it necessary to imprison in his own mind while, paradoxically, giving expression to what he is convinced is the outcome of the application of principles that are held in sincerity and applied with an impartiality that is inseparable from the subjective life. The evaluation which he incorporates in his criticism will be his assessment of what all those concerned with the provision of the entertainment of today try to do and how they succeed or fail. He has to be a sieve, and yet a well-developed individual.

It is legitimate for him to make known his own tastes. His evaluations are the results of the application of special knowledge applied under imposed conditions. He cannot, if he would, place himself in the position of each one of hundreds of theatregoers who constitute the audience on the evening during which he functions as critic. He cannot become completely objective. He must think imaginatively of what those hundreds of human beings may be thinking and feeling, and yet embody in his criticism what he himself has been made to think and to feel—and it is certain that his capacity for both thinking and feeling is in advance of that of most members of the audience. He must view the type of entertainment, whatever it is, from all relevant angles, thinking through various minds, and reach his conclusions through his tastes and values, but not be unmindful of the tastes and values of others, also of the place and purpose of dramatic and theatrical entertainment in the times in which he lives and works.

The critic in the theatre must possess sound knowledge of the impersonal things of drama and the stage, the evolution of drama and the types of plays that evolution has caused to be created. He must, too, know a great deal about the human beings who, in diverse ways, make their contributions to theatrical and dramatic entertainment. He theorizes when assessing the values that are inherent in their respective activities; imagines and observes the expressive reactions of those who have been catered for, theoretically or actually; brings into action his own set of first principles of appraisement without being egoistically ruthless or flabby in thought or weak and vacillating in his application of them.

CHAPTER IV

THE CRITIC'S ANALYSIS

ONE whose contributions have made production and performance in the theatre possible is the author of the play. If the theatrical entertainment is not a straight play, the author's place is taken by those responsible for what has been organized to attract the average theatregoer. With the material provided the critic in the theatre is concerned.

There is sharp differentiation between the product of the creative literary artist who expresses himself (or herself) in play form, and of the organizers of manufactured theatrical goods that are offered for sale in the theatre instead of behind a shop window or over a counter. Yet there are similarities.

Few playwrights deliberately embark upon a piece of writing actuated solely by the necessity to respond to the creative urge and without thought of what may or can happen to the written expression that ultimately results from response. True, literary men who have impelled recognition of merit by the qualities of their writings in novels, essays, and verse have, on occasions, turned to playwriting, and have met with a measure of success; but, again, some have tried and failed. Browning and to a lesser extent, Tennyson, are examples, and Shelley's *The Cenci*, acknowledged as a great tragedy, has never been a notable theatrical success.

R. L. Stevenson and W. E. Henley wrote plays in collaboration, but few, if any, critics would aver that their work as playwrights ranks high. Yet the raw material furnished by one of Stevenson's most dramatic stories, *The Ebb-Tide*, was turned most successfully into a play by Donald Pleasance, produced at the 1952 Edinburgh Festival, and, subsequently, introduced to London audiences by the London Club Theatre Group. When H. G. Wells, prolific writer of prose—novels, histories, and the like—began to think in terms of writing for the theatre, he enlisted the aid of St. John Ervine, who had already a reputation as a successful playwright, as collaborator, but the resultant work, *The Wonderful Visit*, produced at St. Martin's in 1921, will be forgotten—or is forgotten—long before Wells's outstanding novels, *Kipps*, *Tono Bungay*, and *The History of Mr. Polly*. When Henry James turned playwright he merely succeeded in demonstrating that a brilliant writer can also be an unmistakable failure—in the theatre.

The critic in the theatre is likely to be more keenly aware than the average theatregoer of the details of the playwright's contribution to the audience's entertainment. This is not meant to suggest that some theatregoers are indifferent to authorship and intent upon amusement without giving a thought to the one who has made a major contribution to it. The average theatregoer is probably aware of the names of West End "stars" in theatreland, and is attracted by them. His awareness may not be as alert and as impelling as is that of his corresponding number whose interest in entertainment is regularly and persistently centred on the cinema, but he will certainly, from time to time, furnish evidence that "big names" are a box-office magnet.

The average theatregoer will decide upon a visit to the theatre because the play at the Aldwych, the Haymarket, the Criterion, the Phoenix, the Savoy, or St. James's has been rumoured to be "a scream," "a smash hit," "most amusing," "awfully funny," or whatever jargon of appreciation happens to be in currency. Some critics in the theatre by their appraisements will have aided the formulation of these public judgments, while others will have expressed themselves differently: whether criticism makes or prevents a commercial success is a recurring subject of discussion that has not as yet produced a conclusive solution of what is really a problem. There is no doubt truth in the contentions that an appraisement that is a warm appreciation can extend and intensify public interest in a play; that a rigorously derogatory criticism of the same play can have a similar effect on the perverse-mindedness of the average theatregoer; that adverse criticism can send the curious-minded to the theatre in order to test the validity of the critic's opinions; that unqualified praise can keep away from the theatre the critically-minded theatregoer who has clear-cut ideas of what he (or she) wants from theatrical management!

"Who is the author?" is a question many book-readers who use the public libraries or the chain libraries can be asked with surprising results. They can give an adequate summary of the story of a book, relate some of the scenes and situations that the author has introduced, say truthfully that they have liked or disliked the book, but not know the author's name. Similarly, there are theatregoers, who "love" or "adore" or "admire" West-End actors and actresses, who can recall play titles and the names of the theatre in which they saw a "thriller," or a play that was "very funny" or "peculiar," but be without any idea of the author's name.

Of these foibles and preferences of the average theatregoer, of these gaps in knowledge and reflections of indifference to relative values, the critic in the theatre is aware. What effect they have upon him is, in part, conditioned by the type of man he is! There is the danger that his consciousness of his own wider and deeper and more specialized knowledge will generate a feeling of superiority. On the other hand, it may just as readily cause him to recognize that he must exercise particular care to communicate his highly specialized knowledge so that it can be easily comprehended by the average theatregoer who cannot and does not wish to appreciate either expertness or specialization.

The critic in the theatre knows, or gets to know, in advance of a visit to the theatre details of the playwright, the play, the producer, the players. He is helped—sometimes amused—by the publicity matter that the commercial organization of theatrical activities makes available. His special knowledge is ready for recall at any time. New names, either those of writers whose work has not been introduced into the theatre before, or of playwrights of other countries whose writings have not broken through national boundaries, on occasions, involve him in research work. It is not suggested, however, that it is absolutely necessary for the critic in the theatre to know the details of the life-story of the playwright whose play he has to appraise in order to make appraisement practicable.

Further, I do not suggest that knowledge of the opinions of specialist writers on the theatre, or of those who have specially concerned themselves with treatises on drama, is necessarily of primary importance in the professional pursuit of the actual practice of criticism. Nevertheless, such knowledge, which need not be included in the essential equipment of many of the present-day critics in the theatre, is of exceptional general interest. Reflection on salient points repays trouble that is taken to indulge it.

Knowledge of a playwright's way of life can be useful background information. It can illumine the author's intention, with which the critic must seriously concern himself. In relatively few cases does the critic find playwrights as specifically helpful as was Bernard Shaw when he wrote (in the preface to *The Showing-up of Blanco Posnet*): "I am not an ordinary playwright in general practice. I am a specialist in immoral and heretical plays. My reputation has been gained by my persistent struggle to force the public to reconsider its morals. In particular I regard much current morality as to economic and sexual doctrines as disastrously wrong; and I regard certain doctrines of the Christian religion as understood in England to-day with abhorrence. I write plays with the deliberate object of converting the nation to my opinions in these matters. I have no other effectual incentive to write plays, as I am not dependent on the theatre for my livelihood. If I were prevented from producing immoral and heretical plays, I should cease to write for the theatre, and propagate my views from the platform and through books."

Shaw began his playwriting career in collaboration with William Archer, but quickly found that the best way for him was to rely upon himself. The two were concerned in the creation of *Widowers' Houses*, but Shaw soon proved to be too voracious a consumer of the raw material that Archer supplied. Whether Shaw's incentive to write plays was the right incentive, and whether the results of his responses to his incentive were the best, are issues that sharply divide opinions. Since his declaration of his intentions as a playwright scores of books, studies, interpretations dealing with G.B.S. and his works have been published. My reading of these, and of the re-valuations that have appeared since his death in 1950, has served to emphasize the significance of individualism in criticism!

George Bernard Shaw was not the only playwright who helped, or tried to help, people to understand. Another playwright with a long series of successes in the theatre, W. Somerset Maugham, reviewing the period (1915–27) during which he wrote plays in quick succession, stated:[1] "I had by then made up my mind on many things connected with the drama. One of the conclusions I had come to was that a prose play was scarcely less ephemeral than a news sheet. The playwright and the journalist need very similar gifts, a quick eye for a good story and a telling point, animation and a vivid way of writing. All the dramatist needs besides is a specific knack. I do not know that anyone has been able to discover what this knack consists of. It cannot be learnt. It can exist without education or culture. It is a faculty that enables the playwright so to put words that they carry across the footlights and to tell a story, as it were stereoscopically, so that it visibly moves before an audience. It is a very rare faculty: that is why dramatists are so much more highly paid than other artists. It has nothing to do with literary ability, as we know from the fact that the most distinguished novelists have generally failed lamentably when they have tried to write plays. It is a faculty, like that of being able to play by ear, of no spiritual importance. But without it, though your ideas may be profound, your theme original and your characterization acute, you will never be able to write a play. . . . The best way of learning how to write a play is to see one of your own produced. That will teach you how to write lines that the actors find easy to say and, if you have an ear, how far you can carry the rhythm of a sentence without losing the spontaneity of conversation. It will show you what sort of speech and what sort of scene are effective. But I think the secret of play-writing can be given in two maxims: stick to the point and wherever you can, cut."

These quotations are introduced with a specific purpose. The first is direct self-confession; the second, opinion based on experience. Both are by successful writers whose plays cannot be disregarded by any who take a serious interest in the development of British drama, and among the most

[1] *The Summing Up.*

serious-minded of these is the critic in the theatre. Shaw, according to Maugham, with whom critics in many countries are in agreement, exercised an influence on the English stage that has been devastating; Maugham, according to himself, was never a propagandist-playwright. Nevertheless, during his playwriting career, he, too, came under the influence of the arch-propagandist Shaw. "One can scarcely think of St. John Hankin, Stanley Houghton, Somerset Maugham, or even Galsworthy, independently of the moulding influence of Shaw. The late Olive Schreiner and Sarah Grand, both famous novelists, acknowledged Shaw as 'the Master'."[1]

Shaw and Maugham represented with distinction an era that is passing. Shaw himself was largely instrumental in crystallizing the spirit of it. For him the play of ideas was the type of theatrical entertainment that could, appropriately, be provided for a growing, but largely uneducated, democracy. For Maugham, the play *qua* play was the pre-requisite. Shaw's faith held, even after he had attained the age of ninety. *Buoyant Billions*, first produced abroad and subsequently performed at the Malvern Festival of 1949, was, in generous measure, characteristically re-hashed material that was first used by him in his earlier plays, *Getting Married*, *Man and Superman*, *The Apple Cart*, etc. Maugham, when a septuagenarian, saw or thought he saw, a decline in the influence of the play of ideas.

The Play of Ideas

During 1950 members of the oncoming generation, not the youngest, but representative of the playwriting successes that were registered between the two World Wars and subsequently, expressed their opinions on the play of ideas. They differed, on important points, with their leaders. Some of their views, published in *The New Statesman and Nation*, will have been noted by the critic in the theatre today—

> I believe that the best plays are about people and not about things. I am in fact a heretic from the now widely held faith that a play which concerns itself with, say, the artificial insemination of human beings or the National Health Service is of

[1] *Bernard Shaw: Playboy and Prophet.*

necessity worthier of critical esteem than a play about, say, a mother's relations with her son or about a husband's jealousy of his wife.

I further believe that the intellectual *avant-garde* of the English theatre—or rather, let's be both brave and accurate, and say of the English-speaking theatre, since in my view, the Americans are the worst offenders—are, in their insistence on the superiority of the play of ideas over the play of character and situation, not only misguided but old-fashioned. . . .

The theatre of ideas . . . could not, in Shaw's view, live in peace and amity with any other kind of theatre at all. It had to conquer or die.

Well, it conquered all right, and the theatre it had defeated was condemned to death, without benefit, even of a Nürnberg; but, though duly hanged in opprobrium, it strangely refused to die. Why? That surely is a question that should exercise the *avant-garde*.[1]

It is always dismaying when Wilkes declares that he himself is not a Wilkesite. But it should not have surprised Rattigan nor escaped his notice that Shaw, as a congenital artist, [was] for nearly three-quarters of a century the most unreliable of propagandists, even as a pamphleteer or platform speaker, let alone within the sacred precincts of the theatre, where he so scrupulously and wholeheartedly gave the devil his due that it was decades before the public, only gradually inured to this novelty, could understand what the devil he was writing about. It is this liberation from the formula of propagandist or "ideological" play-writing, for which Shaw, almost single-handed, was responsible, in which Rattigan, Bridie and I can now stretch ourselves, bound only by our own limitations, and for which, as Bridie says, we should all be duly grateful.[2]

The thoughts of a creative artist about his medium are, inevitably, an amalgam of pride and prejudice. They are usually passionate, interesting and irresponsible. The thoughts of a critic are usually less passionate, less interesting, and even more irresponsible . . . Shaw was right to attack Shakespeare. Rattigan was right to attack Shaw. Bridie was right to attack Rattigan. I am right to attack the lot of them. The next man will be right to attack me, and may the next man win (as if he could!). . . . The tragedy of Shakespeare is the tragedy of doubt. The comedy of Shaw is the comedy of conviction. Personally I find doubt more convincing. . . . I lack the contemporary faith which proclaims that a spade is a spade, a vitamin, a

[1] Terence Rattigan.
[2] Benn W. Levy.

vitamin, and a windmill, a windmill. I am Quixotic enough to
believe that things are rarely what they seem, and I am content
to leave rules and regulations to those more intellectually
coherent than I, in the confident knowledge that they will
contradict each other at every turn. I trust implicitly in the
limited sincerity of them all, however, and am as interested as
they to see what such excellent individual talents as Terry
Rattigan, James Bridie, and Christopher Fry will be hatching
presently in the necessary isolation of their studies. What they
write is more important than what they think, because we can
usually guess what they think from what they write, while some
of them can write very well without seeming to think at all.
Amen.[1]

We'd have to get ideas out of life before we could remove them
from the drama. Indeed the very first glimmer of the conception
for a play is an idea. There's hardly a thing written as a play, a
novel, or a poem, that hasn't an idea under it, hovering over it,
or in its very core. Life is constantly pummelling itself with ideas
from morn till midnight. No one can write about ideas without
creating persons to express them; but it is one thing to have an
idea in a head and quite another to place it in a play. It takes a
master-mind to do that so that it will appeal to the imagination of
an audience. Shaw and Ibsen are masters of this fancy. . . .
Things change life as well as thought—the railway, the motor-
car, the tractor, the harvest-combine, and even the proletarian
bicycle. A new kind of life is with us, whether we like it or not.
And a good deal of this life will flood into the theatre. The
stalls that give rest to the bums hidden in satin and silk will soon
be ghosts of the past; and the new life will demand new plays
that deal with and interpret the life it lives. And here comes a
pause. The plays written around the new life must be currents
in the mainstream of drama, must be an offspring of the great
tradition. When we decide, instead of playing at being kings or
queens or cavaliers, to play at being proletarians, then let us
play at being them, and not send them forth as lecturers in an
academy hall, preachers in a pulpit, or speakers from a political
platform, important as these activities can be. The dramatist
must see poetry in the smoky hub-bub of a tavern, just as he may
see it in the stately ceremonial of a cathedral, though he may
realize that, while the life in a tavern is always real, that of the
cathedral is often a sham.[2]

Opera taught me to shape my plays into recitatives, arias,
duets, trios, ensemble finales, and bravura pieces to display the

---

[1] Peter Ustinov.
[2] Sean O'Casey.

technical accomplishments of the executants, with the quaint result that all the critics, friendly and hostile, took my plays to be so new, so extraordinary, so revolutionary, that *The Times* critic declared that they were not plays at all as plays had been defined for all time by Aristotle. The truth was that I was going back atavistically to Aristotle, to the tribune stage, to the circus, to the didactic Mysteries, to the word music of Shakespeare, to the forms of my idol Mozart, and to the stage business of the great players whom I had actually seen acting, from Barry Sullivan, Salvini, and Ristori to Coquelin and Chaliapine. I was . . . the most old-fashioned playwright outside China and Japan. But I knew my business both historically and by practice as playwright and producer; . . . without knowing it historically and studying critically the survivals of it that are still in practice —for instance the Westminster School performances of the ancient Latin drama where the women's parts are played by boys as Shakespeare's women's parts were, and are so effective that Shakespeare must have been as strongly against having them played by women as any Holy Willie. No playwright can be fully qualified, nor any theatre critic know what he is pontificating about. And so I close, I hope, this series of essays started by Mr. Rattigan, all of them entertaining in their way, but containing no convincing evidence that the writers have ever seen, written or produced a play.[1]

The play of ideas has many facets. Directly or indirectly, it is propagandist in degree, slight or marked, in presentation— in understatement, in emphasis, in spirit, in interpretation, in reception. A play, succinctly defined, is a story told in dialogue. It may be spoken from the stage, published in book form, uttered as conversation. It is almost certain, from some angle, to have idea-content that can be construed as propaganda. It is easy to read into some of the plays of W. Somerset Maugham, the avowed non-propagandist, matter that is of propaganda value. This attitude, I am aware, brushes aside the dictionary definition of propaganda: "Any association, systematic scheme, or concerted movement for the propagation of a particular doctrine or practice." It is, however, obvious that much that has been considered to be free of propaganda in plays, in volumes, in modern journalism, in discussion circles, in lectures before literary societies, even in university lectures, has influenced appreciably the creation and development of

[1] Bernard Shaw.

ideas, which, in expression, have undermined and weakened established institutions to such an extent that they are in process of disintegration.

John Galsworthy was thought of by some as a propagandist because some of the themes of his plays and his treatment of them were not considered to be "quite proper" when introduced to the conventionally-minded public through the medium of the theatre: *Joy*, which the dramatist describes as "A play on the letter I," makes the point that "when it is ourselves it is always a special case"—in other words, that we are always willing to make excuses to justify our actions, that we are often guilty of lying to excuse our own special cases; *Strife*, a classic of its kind, with industrial strife, the Capital *v*. Labour war, for its theme; *Justice* with its treatment of something larger than the personal issue—the working of the machinery of the law; *The Eldest Son*, with its resemblance to Stanley Houghton's *Hindle Wakes*—a reminder that there are two codes of morality and an echo of his first play, *The Silver Box*, once described as "practically flawless" from the viewpoint of technique; *The Skin Game*, poising, even in balanced treatment, the issue of conflicting ethical codes.

By others Galsworthy was looked upon as a playwright who was too impartial, too well-balanced, too penetrating, a teller of too much truth, too much occupied with the pros and cons of every case and its faithful presentation, to make either a widely popular appeal or an effective propagandist. Years ago Miss Sheila Kaye-Smith in her study of him "placed" him:[1] "He stands midway between the purely literary and the purely popular playwright, and he also occupies middle ground between drama which is entirely for instruction and that which is for amusement only. Poles apart on the one hand from the light comedies of H. H. Davies and Somerset Maugham, he has very little in common with stage preachers such as Shaw and Barker. More polished and more subtle than Houghton, he is less clear-eyed and heroic than Masefield. Undoubtedly his most striking quality as a dramatist is his sense of form and craft, but he is far removed from that school of playwrights, of which Pinero and H. A. Jones are leaders,

[1] *John Galsworthy.*

whose technique amounts to little more than a working knowledge of the stage."

The Poet in the Theatre

There is scope for wide differences of opinion on what is and what is not propagandist matter in play form; also on the near and distant future of the play of ideas. If Maugham is right in his contention that it has outlived its day, and equally right in his suggestion that the poet must be permitted to return to the theatre, what kind of play is likely to be written and produced in the modern theatre? Ronald Peacock has written provocatively on the subject. Considering the play of ideas in relation to the effects of Ibsen, he states:[1] "In his histories, in the plays with an almost autobiographical element, *Brand* and *Peer Gynt*, in the plays of the last period, Ibsen is most dramatic and most poetic at one and the same time. The work of the middle period is highly dramatic, but the creative imagination is subordinated to a critical analysis in the cause of truthfulness. It is the work that had an immense influence on the drama in Europe. Under the impact of this subject-matter that had a pronounced contemporary interest, a controversial value, and a social application, writing and production in the English theatre burst into a great efflorescence; and yet the movement failed to produce great dramatic literature. That is the remarkable fact and the critical problem. The novelty and immediacy of the subject-matter, and the conscientious temper of the new writers, were clearly notable and warranted all the excitement they caused. It seemed that the theatre was being liberated effectively from stereotyped entertainment, and art rescued from the aestheticism of the 'nineties'; and if vitality is to be measured by these things and by extent of production and imitation, the new type of play would certainly claim that quality. It attained a front position for itself. For a generation the most widely accepted notion of what a good play should be was a thoughtful play for thoughtful people. From Shaw and Granville-Barker, through eminent and minor playwrights alike, and not forgetting the timely assistance of reflective rational Euripides, who was played as

[1] *The Poet in the Theatre.*

often as anyone else, down to a recent work like *Thunder Rock*, in which we see a last low ebbing of the tide, the type has dominated the stage and criticism. Looking back now on the period that produced *The Voysey Inheritance* and *Candida*, *Loyalties* and *The Skin Game*, *Outward Bound* and *A Bill of Divorcement*, *Young Woodley* and *The Vortex*, *Robert's Wife* and *Dangerous Corner*, it is incredible that it should ever have been called 'great.' All these plays are competent, some of them excellent; all of them are representative plays of ideas, all successes of their time. Nevertheless they can attract now but little critical interest."

Mr. Peacock's first chapter, quite appropriately in the special circumstances, opens with an evaluation of T. S. Eliot: "Eliot's first great merit in respect of English drama is simply to have challenged a whole period by criticism and practice. The crux of the problem was the lack of poetry and style, and the degree of failure, the continued adherence to false ideas, made it necessary to search afresh for the foundations of the art." Later, he declares: "In taking verse to drama again and drama to verse Eliot made a move of complex significance. It was at once a renovation of verse and a revival of drama. It was a break-away from poetry conceived too exclusively as the expression of the sentient anarchic individual, and a return to the wider conception of it as a presentation of human actions with their reverberations in human society. And it was a restoration to drama of poetic conventions that intensify its 'degree of form,' to use Eliot's own term. The field of verse is widened again; the form of drama is heightened."

What if drama takes the other turning, and accommodates the playwright who thinks in terms of communities and the manifestations and expressions of life as it is lived within them? Think of the American Clifford Odets: "I am no believer in art for art's sake. At least once before I die I would like to write a fine revolutionary play." He draws attention to his methods of preparation for playwriting: ". . . I am for ever clipping items from the newspapers, for ever making copious notes. But I don't remember ever once referring to a clipping when I started writing a scene. However, I find the clippings and notes valuable in the sense that they set up in me unconscious reactions and adjustments to my material. I mean an unconscious distillation takes place. Your 'it could have happened' is the result."

The playwright's task is self-imposed. His idea for a play gives rise to a theme which is dealt with in story form through dialogue. Thus he is involved in construction suitable, as he thinks, to give effect to his intention. The result, which may or may not satisfy him, is one of the concerns of the critic in the theatre, but there cannot be exclusive concentration on it. The playwright himself is not always clear about either his intention or his fulfilment. He may know what he wants to achieve, but lack the ability satisfactorily to catch and to hold his idea in play form. The critic is seldom in a position to know exactly what passed through the playwright's mind during the period of his creativeness, but he has to clarify his own opinions on what was attempted and what achieved. And, naturally, his own opinions, notwithstanding his special knowledge and skill and experience in the application of it, are often at variance with the opinions that are expressed by his critic-colleagues, each of whom can be credited with the possession of similar qualifications for the performance of his specialist task.

Farquhar has it (*A Discourse Upon Comedy*): "Now here are twenty criticks . . . and yet every one is a critick after his own way; that is, such a play is best because I like it. A very familiar argument, methinks, to prove the excellence of a play, and to which an author would be very unwilling to appeal for his success."

Playwrights as human beings prefer their plays to be praised rather than condemned, although as practising playwrights some of them may profess an indifference to professional criticism, opining that they know better than the critics. It is possible for the playwright to be so self-satisfied and self-confident, so indifferent to the opinions of others, so certain that what he has done is, if not the best that can be done, at any rate, as good as is necessary for practical purposes, that he can ignore criticism.

It is impossible, however, for the critic in the theatre to ignore the work of the playwright whose task has been performed before his play is brought to life on the stage for the

entertainment of theatregoers. The critic's starting-point of
evaluation is his analysis of the play *qua* play. He may be out
of sympathy with the playwright's intention in writing the
play, have no difficulty in arriving at the honest opinion that
the play might very well have remained unwritten for any
qualitative values that he, as a citizen, in active antagonism
to the creed, or dogma, or policy for which the playwright
stands, can discern in it, but as a critic he has to assess the
play not only in terms of ideas, but also of theme, story, construction, characterization, theatrical effectiveness, etc. The
more serious the play, the more exacting is the critic's task,
but, even when the entertainment is not intended to be taken
as anything other than amusing theatrical entertainment, he
has to think of it from sundry angles, including its effectiveness
as what it purports to be, theatrical entertainment.

When the playwright "knows little or nothing about his
own play"—a summing up of some authors by Sydney W.
Carroll, who in the heyday of his professional life was one of
the outstanding dramatic critics of the time—it is necessary
for others, the producer, the actors and actresses, to interpret
it, and then for the critic in the theatre to appraise the collective
work in performance. The task can be exceedingly difficult.
For example, a creative literary artist does not always know
why he himself wrote certain passages, or, having written the
passages, what he intended them to convey. This type of
writing rarely gets itself embedded in play form, although there
are lines in polemical or paradoxical plays, some of Shaw's
plays, for example, or in poetic drama or plays in verse—some
would cite T. S. Eliot's *The Cocktail Party* illustratively—which
call for discussion as a preliminary to understanding.

The Author's Intention

If the playwright does not know what he was driving at
when he wrote a particular play, or if he has failed to communicate the clarity of his own mind because of faulty workmanship, or if, as can happen, a character in development has
caused the creative playwright, perhaps against his desire, to
alter his proposed story, treatment, and conclusion, the critic
in the theatre cannot plead obscurity, confusion, or uncertainty

in the mind of the playwright as an excuse for obscurity, confusion, and uncertainty in his own pronouncements on the play. His opinions must be soundly founded and firmly expressed. The beginning of his understanding is his clear understanding of the author's intention:[1] "The producer who knows his job, whatever may be his height of brow, the producer (whether of farce, Greek tragedy, modern comedy, no matter what the medium may be) sees that every ounce of content is brought to the attention of the audience, and to every individual member of that audience. For want of a better phrase let us call that content 'the author's intention.' What did the author mean at this or that point? What does *this* bear in relation to *that*? and above all, what relation does *this* and *that* bear to the other? . . . When I go to see a Galsworthy play I want the Galsworthy intention, and if I go to see a modern comedy, I do not want vaudeville. . . . The recognition of this principle of the author's intention is one that cannot be too highly emphasized. It is the whole keynote of everything that arises from a play. If not thoroughly understood and applied, the whole art of the theatre falls to the ground and the art of production becomes a sort of false pretences in the theatre."

Linked with understanding of the author's intention is the art of appraisement. The critic in the theatre is called upon, among other things, to pronounce judgment on the play as a play. What is a good play? "The play that is theatrically effective and entertaining" is one reply, relevant but inadequate. A play in performance can be "good theatre"— and pernicious, subversive, superficial, salacious. It can, too, be sincere with sincerity emphasizing, from an angle different from that adopted by the playwright through the medium of his characters, what the average theatregoer may, from his point of view, rightly consider are "the wrong things." It can be a competent piece of workmanship, undistinguished, however, by brilliance, or even great skill in marshalling and discharging worth-while thoughts through dialogue. It can be weak as a written play, but strong in its appeal when it is expertly produced and performed by talented players.

[1] F. E. Doran in *Theatre and Stage.*

To dodge rather than to wrestle with the problem of accurate and adequate definition, and to declare that a play is "a story told from the stage" does not suffice. What is presented on the stage may be a trite, tawdry, tedious story, and remain a play, but triteness, tawdriness, and tediousness are relative, and cannot at all times be made applicable to all. A platitude to one who knows much that is relevant to the subject of the platitude is something entirely different to the ignoramus or the adolescent or adult with slight knowledge of the subject, and with weak powers of correlation and deduction. Similarly, a play that the expert-specialist in drama and the theatre considers to be an unworthy play can be rightly considered by the average theatregoer to be a praiseworthy play. "Good," "weak," "dull," "commonplace," "boring," and other qualitative adjectives are used cautiously not only by the conscientious critic in the theatre but also by others who are disinclined to attach descriptive labels to plays that can, legitimately, be variously evaluated by playgoers.

When the playwright begins his work he can elect to set out on one of a number of routes that he can take. He may find no difficulty in making his initial choice and create for himself great difficulties in keeping to the chosen route. There are more ways than one to take him to his destination, of which, indeed, at the outset he may be unconscious. I recall some pertinent writing by John Galsworthy in his essay entitled "Some Platitudes Concerning Drama":[1] "It was once said of Shakespeare that he had never done any good to any one, and never would. This, unfortunately, could not, in the sense in which the word 'good' was then meant, be said of most modern dramatists. In truth, the good that Shakespeare did to humanity was of a remote, and, shall we say, eternal nature; something of the good that men get from having the sky and the sea to look at. And this partly because he was, in his greater plays at all events, free from the habit of drawing a distorted moral. Now, the playwright who supplies to the public the facts of life distorted by the moral which it expects, does so that he may do the public what he considers an immediate good, by fortifying its prejudices; and the dramatist

[1] *The Inn of Tranquillity.*

who supplies to the public facts distorted by his own advanced morality, does so because he considers that he will at once benefit the public by substituting for its worn-out ethics, his own. In both cases the advantage the dramatist hopes to confer on the public is immediate and practical.

"But matters change, and morals change; men remain— and to set men, and the facts about them, down faithfully, so that they draw for us the moral of their natural actions, may also possibly be of benefit to the community. It is, at all events, harder than to set men and facts down, as they ought, or ought not to be. This, however, is not to say that a dramatist should, or indeed can, keep himself and his temperamental philosophy out of his work. As a man lives and thinks, so will he write. But it is certain, that to the making of good drama, as to the practice of every other art, there must be brought an almost passionate love of discipline, a white-heat of self-respect, a desire to make the truest, fairest, best thing in one's power; and that to these must be added an eye that does not flinch. Such qualities alone will bring to a drama the selfless character which soaks it with inevitability."

I have quoted Galsworthy partly because, as I have suggested, what are platitudes to one are flashes of genius to another. One primary aim of the critic in the theatre from the moment the curtain goes up on the performance of a play is to do his best to understand the author's intention.

Attention has necessarily been fixed on the appraisement of what can conveniently be classified as "straight" plays in performance. The critic in the theatre who must write about entertainment that is designed to appeal to the eyes and ears, but not necessarily to the brain in ways that test its fitness to analyse the expression of thoughts and to follow analysis by logical deductions, must, none the less, seek for and convince himself that he has found the author's, or the manufacturer's, or the purveyor's, or the team's (or whatever the appropriate word may be) intentions.

Spectacular shows, musical medleys, operatic offerings, and other legitimate forms of theatrical entertainment, including ballet and dancing, the critic in the theatre must deal with from time to time, but he is not necessarily the critic whose regular task is to appraise "straight" plays. He, too, will be a specialist, with special knowledge of branches of dramatic and theatrical art, but his starting-point will be similar to that of his colleague who is concerned with "straight" plays: what does this particular form of theatrical entertainment set out to do; how is it done; is it worth while?

The critic in the theatre, in whatever branch of criticism he specializes, requires to be expert in analysis. The theatrical entertainment that satisfies the requirements of sound criticism does so because each component has been moulded and shaped to make it a suitable integral part of the whole. Each part is assessed separately by the critic, who is then in a position to appraise the whole, no relevant part having been omitted from his analysis.

CHAPTER V

THE CRITIC'S REACTIONS

THE critic in the theatre, trying to make sure that he understands, clearly and thoroughly, the author's intention, arrives at a reasoned opinion on how the playwright has performed his task of playwriting. There can be sharply defined clashes of opinion. The playwright may be well satisfied with his work, but his satisfaction may arise out of his unsatisfactory functioning as a self-critic, and it may not be shared by the critic.

There is no such human being as an infallible critic. The critic's deductive reasoning about the author's intention may be wrong. Even when that intention is crystal clear, the manner in which it has been implemented may create doubts. Science has not reached the stage at which it enables man to declare soundly and with finality that in a given set of circumstances a human being will, with certainty, react in speech and behaviour strictly in accordance with scientific theory and expectations. Obviously, therefore, the playwright in his manipulation of characters may be satisfied that he has made each character convincing in itself and also in relation to all the other characters, but the critic in the theatre, having to theorize about, and to form opinions on, the playwright's interplay of characters can reasonably, but either rightly or wrongly, be dissatisfied—hence the differences of opinion that are revealed by a comparison of criticisms, written by a number of thoroughly expert critics, of a specific play.

The playwright, having done or failed to do what he had in mind when he wrote, passes on his play to others, whose task is to breathe life into it for the entertainment of the average theatregoer. One important intermediary between playwright and audience in the modern theatre is the director or producer. He has two sets of "raw material" on which to work: (1) the material of the play; and (2) the players, in order to give life, point, and purpose to the public performance of imaginative writing that he is expected to interpret in terms of truth to author and pleasure and significance to the audience. His work has to be assessed by the critic in the theatre. It is work that has been done behind the scenes before the public presentation of the play, and that is brought to the notice of the audience through the individual and collective work of actors, actresses, stage director, designers, electricians, stage manager, and assistants; in short, by a team of artists and workers, complementary and each understanding the relationship of parts to whole.

Norman Marshall, in his Foreword to Hal D. Stewart's *Stagecraft*, written from the stage director's viewpoint, gives in detail the reminder that when the curtain rises on a first night the producer hands over his production to the care of the stage director, adding that during the next two or three hours a poor stage director can easily make a highly-finished production seem careless, untidy, and under-rehearsed.

The Producer

The producer's task is onerous. Like the critic in the theatre on the first night, he may have had difficulty in convincing himself of the soundness of his interpretation of the author's intention. He will, however, have had to take practical action, to give artistic, theatrical, and effective purpose to public performance during the rehearsal preparation for it. The script of the play may or may not help him. In some cases he will be assisted by the author himself. The assistance may be personal. The author himself may be a successful playwright and a man of the theatre who can teach players (and others) how, by exercising the art of acting, they can register desired effects. Bernard Shaw at the height of his career (and afterwards) was a playwright who made personal contributions to the theatrical effectiveness of the presentation of his plays. He knew not only what he wanted, but also how to instruct others so that they were able to do as he wished, which was often far more effective than anything that would have been read into the play and the playing of it by the most experienced and imaginative producer. Similar remarks apply to Noel Coward, whose playwriting, producing, and playing have recurringly revealed him as a specialist in each of several roles.

The producer who can enlist the personal assistance of the playwright is perhaps fortunate. It all depends . . .

An indirect form of personal assistance may also be appreciated. An actor or actress who turns playwright does not, when writing a play, necessarily apply his or her practical knowledge of the art of acting, but it is probable that, when a producer is confronted with the task of handling a play that has been written by a former or a practising player, the parts will be written with a keener sense of stage requirements than is often revealed by the academic, literary-minded playwright who thinks of the stage in terms of the study, and makes surer of his matter than of the manner in which it is presented in its play form. Sir Arthur Pinero, who wrote many theatrical successes at the turn of the century and before the First World War, was an actor who turned playwright.

The Printed Play

Henry Arthur Jones, whose name is often linked with that of Pinero, in an inaugural address that he delivered at the re-opening of the City of London College on 12th October, 1893, speaking of the relations of the drama and education, contended that:[1] ". . . there is in the drama an immense power of inculcating a wide knowledge of life. . . . No book, no other art, no mere spoken address, no system of education can so instantly and vividly burn and brand the memory with the realities of life, and leave them for ever stamped and pictured in the chambers of imagery, as can the acted play." He was not, however, concerned solely with "the acted play." The year before he was expounding his individualistic views on "The Literary Drama." It should be conceded, he pleaded, "that the art of writing modern English drama is, or should be, an intellectual art. . . . My only desire is to obtain some recognition and definite status for the art of play-writing. . . . Surely the best, perhaps the only, safeguard against the success of all kinds of bunkum and clap-trap on the English stage is the custom of publishing our plays."

[1] *The Renascence of the English Drama.*

Since Jones's advocacy, the practice of printing plays has been developed, but not, one suspects, to guarantee the publishers an adequate reward for their enterprise in giving permanent form to the ephemeral traffic of the stage that is represented by the public performance of plays. The outcome of this practice has, however, been of practical assistance to sundry types of workers in the theatre, including the critic. He can, on occasions, study the printed play before he attends the performance of it that he must appraise; or, having seen a play in performance, confirm or contradict his own opinions by analytical study of the printed version of the play before his own criticism must appear in print.

Help for the producer may be obtained from the printed page. He is concerned not only with the production of new plays to which he himself by his work will help to give life for the first time, but also with revivals of old plays. If he has undertaken to produce a play by Shakespeare or by any other of the Elizabethans, examples of classical drama, plays of historical significance, etc., he will have the literature of the theatre and drama for reference and research purposes. In some cases there will be available the equivalent of a small library of the writings of commentators, interpreters, and specialist-appraisers of different kinds. When the producer is interested professionally in the revival of a modern play by an established playwright, the probability is that the printed text will be obtainable and that the stage directions will be much fuller than any that can be found in the printed versions of older plays.

Go for illustrative examples to Barrie's *The Admirable Crichton*, Act I; Galsworthy's *The Silver Box*, Act I, Sc. 1; Granville-Barker's *Waste*, Act I; Shaw's *Back to Methuselah*, Act I; Noel Coward's *The Vortex*, Act I; J. B. Priestley's *Johnson Over Jordon*, Act I.

All these plays have significance for the student of the evolution of English drama. Some of the directions demonstrate the desire of some playwrights to make the printed play attractive as reading matter—more attractive than it was made before systematic methods to popularize the publication and the reading of plays were adopted. Compare the opening direction of *The Admirable Crichton* with that of *The Silver Box*;

note the psychological content of the direction for *Waste*, the scope offered by Shaw's direction for the setting for the first part of *Back to Methuselah*, and the significance of Mr. Priestley's note.

When printed plays give full stage directions, the producer is likely to have more detailed guidance than he has when he handles the first play of an unknown author or a play that is in typescript, the playwright leaving interpretation to the expert who is responsible for the production of his play. At best the opening direction will strike the keynote of what begins to take place immediately the curtain goes up; other directions repeat or alter the note, but when taken in totality it is possible for the producer to misconstrue them unwittingly, although his intentions are to interpret them scientifically, either to reveal truthful facets of life that are caught up and reflected by the characters in action or to secure the effects that are inherent in the dialogue and business and be faithful to them.

The ideal producer is difficult to find, but he or she may exist.

Attention focused on the producer brings out his importance in relation to the playwright on the one hand and to the players and through them to the audience on the other. He may or may not misinterpret the author's intentions. If he does, he will fail to present the play that the author wrote, but failure on these lines may not be an injustice to the playwright. A producer, by handling the play with inspiration, imagination, skill, and understanding, bringing into play abundance of technical knowledge that he has acquired in practical experience, can sometimes extract more that is good and effective in the play than the playwright himself appreciates is in it.

The Critic's Difficult Task

It follows from what has been recalled and emphasized that the critic in the theatre has a difficult task when, in the first place, he attempts to reach a serious opinion on the play as a whole; in short, he considers the playwright's idea, theme, story, construction, intention, and fulfilment, and proceeds to assess the contributions that are made at rehearsals under the influence and authority of the producer, and during the performance by the players whose art in action creates reactions in the audience. His difficulty is, undoubtedly, increased by the pivotal work that has been done by the producer during rehearsals. Some of the aids that are available for the producer can also be used by the critic. For example, he can obtain a copy of a printed play as easily as can the producer, but he may encounter obstacles when the play is unpublished.

Inquiries that he may deem it desirable to make before he is present at the first night may elicit useful information, which, ordinarily, would not come into his possession. However, when he has done everything that he can reasonably be expected to do in advance of engaging in the actual task of evaluation during a play's performance, he will have to answer for himself questions which he will ask himself and which will not or cannot be answered for him.

As one member of the theatre audience, albeit an expert member, he is not in a position to know for certain whether every effect is the effect that the producer wished the players to register; whether the dialogue is handled in every detail in accordance with the producer's instructions and guidance; whether movement, deportment, business, are what the producer had in mind and made known he wanted when he controlled the players in rehearsal.

Assuming that the producer is fully satisfied with every detail of a performance—an assumption as generous as unwise —the critic in the theatre will not know whether all the details of what the producer required and achieved are in harmony with the playwright's legitimate intentions and aesthetic tastes. One illustration of what is involved in the critic's task must serve.

Stage speech is of great importance in sound characterization. ". . . the speech of an actor," states Edwin C. White,[1] "should seem to be the natural speech of the character, and it is undoubtedly proper for him to interpret his character, but in doing so he must at the same time be distinct, and audible. This . . . is the actor's first duty."

Speech alone, even the effective use of speech, is only one of

[1] *Problems of Acting and Play Production.*

a number of essentials for sound characterization. Without
speech, however, most characters in most plays during most
of their time on the stage would be unable to communicate
the playwright's intentions—and with speech it is easy for
communication to be falsified. Think, for example, of
Doolittle's lines in the second act of Shaw's *Pygmalion*—

> Dont say that, Governor. Dont look at it that way. What am
> I, Governors both? I ask you, what am I? I'm one of the
> undeserving poor: thats what I am. Think of what that means
> to a man. It means that hes up agen middle class morality all
> the time. If theres anything going, and I put in for a bit of it,
> it's always the same story "Youre undeserving; so you cant have
> it." But my needs is as great as the most deserving widow's that
> ever got money out of six different charities in one week for the
> death of the same husband. I dont need less than a deserving
> man: I need more. I dont eat less hearty than him: and I
> drink a lot more. I want a bit of amusement, cause I'm a
> thinking man. I want cheerfulness and a song and a band when
> I feel low. Well, they charge me just the same for everything as
> they charge the deserving. What is middle class morality?
> Just an excuse for never giving me anything. Therefore, I ask
> you, as two gentlemen, not to play that game on me. I'm playing
> straight with you. I aint pretending to be deserving. I'm un-
> deserving; and I mean to go on being undeserving. I like it;
> and thats the truth. Will you take advantage of a man's nature
> to do him out of the price of his own daughter what hes brought
> up and fed and clothed by the sweat of his brow until shes growed
> big enough to be interesting to you two gentlemen? Is five
> pounds unreasonable? I put it to you; and I leave it to you.

Nuance, music, rhythm, flow, meaning, pertinence,
emphasis, dialect, rhetoric, and other aspects of speech used
for interpretation enter into the correct and appropriate
delivery of these lines on the stage. Members of the audience
will understand these readily if they are convinced by the
actor of Shaw's characteristic lucidity and mastery of dialogue
for effective stage speech. The critic must react to them, as,
indeed, he must to every detail of production and performance.
He is capable of evaluating them. He may decide that the
actor who plays the part of Doolittle could not have uttered
any of the words with more telling and appropriate theatrical
effect, and award, mentally, full marks for the delivery. He
can assume that the producer (or the actor) decided upon the

final style of utterance (pronunciation, articulation, pace, phrasing, etc.), but he will not know whether the foundations of his assumption are solid and sound. If they are, he will, if he desires, praise either the producer or the actor, probably the latter.

When the critic in the theatre is convinced that speech from the stage has been misused or abused, with resultant falsification of meaning and distortion of spirit, he may, unwittingly, blame the actor for conscientious work carried out in accordance with the producer's rigorous imposition of his own individualized, perhaps unjustifiably obstinate, opinions. This illustration can reasonably be alleged to be an exaggeration, a bad example of something that never happens on the professional—or even the amateur—stage! A delicate balancing of the pros and cons of the allegation is unnecessary. The illustration serves as a reminder of the essentiality of the critic's reaction to production and play-points, major and minor. He has to be both a theorist, speculating about aims and attainments, and an exerciser of the critical faculty on issues of facts and matters of taste. He must, in addition to understanding and interpreting the playwright's intention and analysing the work that has been done by the producer in order to present the play from the stage, form opinions on the relationship of the producer to the playwright, the players to the producer, and the audience to the players, perhaps on the producer, and certainly on the product of the playwright. In actuality, his seemingly straightforward task at the rise of the curtain becomes, through reaction to components of the whole as the performance proceeds, increasingly complex before the final curtain falls.

CHAPTER VI

THE CRITIC'S ATTITUDE

WHEN Dame Irene Vanbrugh was rehearsing Lady Teazle she bent her head. "Don't do that, you'll shake all the powder off your hair. In a powder period, keep your head rigid always," advised Beerbohm Tree. This advice, says the actress in her autobiography, *To Tell My Story*, gave her "many lights on movements and carriage to that period." She acknowledges the help that she received from other stage personalities: from Henry Irving she "learnt the strength of a still, the power of a silent figure." Sarah Bernhardt showed her "a woman really in love with her stage lover," Dame Madge Kendal "a woman poignantly suffering and the great value of reserve," and Lucien Guitry "among the countless other things, how a speech is never a speech but just an expression of thoughts, how difficult it is to learn a long speech and never let your audience guess for one moment that it is a speech."

Dame Irene Vanbrugh made her first appearance on the stage on 20th August, 1888, as Phoebe in *As You Like It*. When James Agate broadcast a series "Stars in Their Courses," he concluded his tribute to her in these words: "Of her is to be said the one thing which most artists would chiefly wish to have said about them. . . . 'She knows her job'." Had she been taught it or had she acquired her histrionic skill by experience? In her autobiography she explained herself: "I think a great deal can be taught of the simple rules and effects —rules which took me years to discover, I could have learnt in a very short time if the R.A.D.A. had been in existence in my day. Sarah Thorne taught beautifully but told you more how to do a thing than why you should do it." Dame Irene Vanbrugh was a brilliant exponent of English acting as it was when the nineteenth century closed, and an outstanding example of how a playwright—Pinero, whose only serious competitor in the playwriting field for a time was Henry

Arthur Jones—can have his plays carried to conspicuous theatrical success by having a player of distinction available for a pivotal part, and, conversely, how a player can have his or her rise to fame and stardom accelerated by the quality of the parts that a playwright can write specially for him or her. Dame Irene Vanbrugh "created" Rose Trelawney in *Trelawney of the Wells*, Sophie in *The Gay Lord Quex*, Nina Jesson in *His House in Order*, and Zoe Blundell in *Mid-Channel* (among other parts).

Many playwrights have written plays with a part suitable for a particular actress or actor, and, by doing so, have helped themselves and the player to become better known and to achieve fame.

A poor play can be "made" by a first-class actress—but only in a limited sense. Any play is, or should be, greater than its pivotal part, and any player, no matter how far on the road to histrionic fame she or he may have travelled, is at best only one member of a team. The work of the team counts, or should count, far more than any individual's contribution to it, and the producer, recognizing the importance of every member of a cast, does his best to make both the interpretation of each character of the play and the spirit of the performance of the play as a whole as effective as it can be made.

The commerce of the theatre seeks, from time to time, to exploit the personality of an actress or actor and succeeds. Theatrical management is well aware of the magnetism of "the star," and seeks to turn the ordinary, though highly competent, player into an ever-increasing asset as a box-office draw. To this end the commercial man in the theatre has recourse to publicity and advertising methods, and, in addition, he seeks to capitalize not only histrionic talent but also attractive aspects of the private life of either the star in embryo or the star who has arrived and who must be held firmly in the theatregoing public's eye as exceptional and superlative. In consequence, at the creative starting-point of the traffic of the stage, the studio or wherever plays are written—Shaw once said that the majority of his plays had been written in Pitman's Shorthand as he rode in London buses as they stopped and

started in the busy thoroughfares—the playwright may combine
his urge to express himself in play form with the desire to
provide a medium for a first-class actress or actor to demonstrate ability and artistry in interpretation.

At the intermediate stage, where Art at its best or below-
art work that is undertaken with quite legitimate purposes in
mind—profit-making, entertaining the theatregoing public,
preaching a message—the man of commerce is active. On the
one hand he serves the playwright and all those who are concerned with turning play into performance, and on the other
he seeks to bring the theatregoing public into contact with the
performance in order that all may benefit. Also at the intermediate stage is the producer. As a specialist, he knows more
than the average playwright about getting a play on the stage
and across to the audience. He also knows more than the
average player, who can reasonably be expected to be sensitive
to the collective work of members of the cast, but who,
primarily, is likely to be concerned with her or his responsibility for doing the best with the character that has to be
played. However rigorous a player's self-criticism may be, it
is impossible for the subjective self to see every good point or
every bad point through the eyes of the producer. But before
a player need embark upon self-criticism, he must have the
necessary histrionic equipment upon which to draw for acting
purposes. Parenthetically, suitability for a part does not
necessarily ensure choice for the part. Personal and extraneous
factors enter into casting—a fact of life that has to be faced
just as nepotism in other professional or commercial spheres
has often to be accepted as inescapable. But to develop this
line of thought would be to enter into carping and misleading
criticism. The player whose technique is wholly satisfactory,
whose personality is in harmony with requirements, whose
availability for playing is opportune, will succeed in making
her first appearance in the theatre at some stage of her efforts
to adopt acting as her profession. What happens afterwards is
partly the reward of merit, recognition by those who have
power to accelerate, to retard, or to frustrate advancement,
and luck. Lillah McCarthy wrote:[1] "I once heard a famous

[1] *Myself and My Friends.*

dramatic critic—a Frenchman—say: 'The theatre: it is the art of preparation.' He was, of course, thinking of the playwright's art, but what he said is also true of the art of actor or actress.

"There are two types of actress. The professional creed of the one is 'improvisation,' that of the other 'preparation.' The one relies on genius, personality or popularity, the other on hard work; on the genius which is the infinite capacity for taking pains."

What, then, makes a good actor—or actress? The well known Irish actress, the late Sara Allgood, once said that physical strength was the first essential in any player, male or female, and contended that it was useless to think of a stage career if one were weak in body. Review the lives of actors and actresses and it will be noted that in a large number three important characteristics—exceptional vitality, sound health, and high spirits—are common. None of these is easy to cultivate if it is not a natural endowment, although even when Nature itself imposes a handicap something can be done by the individual to effect improvements, to intensify vitality, to take precautionary health measures, to nurture potential into actual good health, and to adopt a philosophy which enables a human being to enjoy life. But for those who would exercise the art of acting, something more than these qualities is requisite.

A few reminders will direct attention to the desirable equipment for the actor, also to some insurmountable handicaps which, paradoxically, can in certain circumstances be turned to professional advantage.

The height of the adult human being is fixed by Nature. Nothing can be done appreciably to modify it. None the less, either exceptional tallness or shortness, although limiting, can be made to serve special ends. The voice is another instrument of Nature. Speech training can effect great improvements, and stage speech, in its many expressions, is of great importance. Dame Sybil Thorndike has written:[1] "In my profession what is said on the stage is often considered to be as important as the manner of saying it, but all who have expert knowledge are

[1] Foreword to *Anthology of Play Scenes, Verse and Prose*—1

very conscious of the importance of both sense and sound."
This is to the point.

Language and Interpretation

The playwright is an expert in the use of language; an artist
in the selection and arrangement of words. Unless he can
write effective dialogue it will be exceedingly difficult, if not
impossible, to give verisimilitude to the delineation of his
characters on the stage. The task of making his characters
"live" has to be undertaken by the players. Therefore they too
must understand language and the purposes for which it is
used. Merely to say on the stage what the playwright has caused
to be printed on the page of a book or written or typed on
paper does not suffice: there must be understanding of word
relationships, of textual significance.

Language that is used by the playwright to express reasoned
thoughts cannot appropriately be said on the stage as though
the language were intended to reveal feelings and emotions.

The player, therefore, must know how to use language to
give weight and purpose, light and shade, relative values,
rhythm and music to the lines that are the player's part. These
lines are not lines in isolation. They are related to what has
gone before and to what follows; parts of the mind of the
character in expression; communications of reactions to
circumstances imaginatively created by the playwright in
dealing with his theme and in telling his story; manufactured
conversations which have to be given the semblance of spontaneous and natural conversation that arises in the commonplace exchange of gossip and ideas.

The clash of personalities in discussion or argument may be
presented, or there may be dialogue that conveys flights of
imagination and the stirrings of the depths.

Much depends upon the type of play in which players act
and what the author's intention in writing the play was, as
interpreted by actors and actresses under the direction and
guidance of the producer. It follows that each word, each
phrase, each line has to be taken contextually. When dialogue
is handled wrongly, falsification easily results. Wrong notes
are struck; balance and poise are destroyed, the underlying

intention of revealing one person's reaction to another's words and deeds is missed histrionically and artistically.

C. E. Montague in his criticism of one presentation of *Hamlet*, which he called "this huge Gothic castle of a poem, with its curious dimnesses, cross lights, confusions almost," said that to act the principal part in it "is like having to sing a lyric that is beautiful in other ways but set with whole constellations of nubbly consonants, which the singer's respect for some cacophonous Browning forbids him to cut or dodge." This brings to mind some of the difficulties with which the players in some of the greatest parts have to contend. The difficulties are of a different order, but no fewer in contemporary comedies.

The idiom of stage speech is subject to fashion as is the jargon of Mayfair or the slang of Covent Garden or Billingsgate. Training to ensure mastery of the voice can be successful, and yet mastery alone will not guarantee sensitive delineation of character on the stage. The producer's aid is often necessary, and even he and his players may not attain artistic ends.

Often during the last few decades the voice of the critic in the theatre has been heard on paper! It has been raised against the modern taste for inaudibility, for the deliberate under-use of the voice on some lines in order to give heightened point to other lines for desired, but often unachieved, artistic purposes. In these circumstances, the players may be expert mistresses or masters of voice and speech control, but have to respect the wishes of the producer with whose views they may disagree but to whose instructions they cannot remain indifferent and, at the same time, remain in the cast. Timing, pace, nuance, attack, emphasis—these, with other specialized usages, have to be understood by the player.

Language and speech interlock. The playwright's sense of the theatre may be stronger than his grip of language. His dialogue may be sufficient to enable him to tell his story, but the manner of his telling may, in comparison with his instinct for the creation of theatrical situations as he deals with his theme, provide evidence of his weakness as a playwright. Whatever the quality of his dialogue is, however, the players must use it, unless the producer is permitted to alter it for the sake of theatrical effectiveness—or amends the dialogue without permission! But danger lies in altering a licensed script and is best avoided. Rehearsals reveal defects, but the fastidious playwright who insists on knowing what is going on in the preparation for the translation of his play from script to stage may remain unconvinced of improvements that are suggested and obstinately take his stand for the retention of the "letter" of his play, leaving the producer, with the aid of the cast, free to do the best he can with its spirit.

The language of the play, its dialogue, and the voices of the players, the instruments with which they communicate the author's intention to the audience, are only two aspects of production with which the producer must be concerned and to which the critic in the theatre must be attentive.

The player has to do more than use his voice. If the producer has a cast with which he is wholly satisfied, if each player is consistent in making the most of his vocal equipment to achieve sound interpretation that is marked by sensitive artistry, both producer and players must also think of visual effects. The voice is important; so, too, is the face. Lips, mouth, eyes, even eyebrows, and nose are brought into play in facial expression, which is a powerful aid in delineation and impression alike. But the components of the player's equipment are more numerous than these features. The manner in which some amateur players shake and in other ways misuse their head, by wrong neck movement, thrusting the head forward in a way that is reminiscent of rigid mechanism in motion, is an almost unnecessary reminder that the player must be body conscious, conscious of his body from the crown of his head to the soles of his feet, and yet use his body, in conjunction with his voice, to convey the impression of a naturalness of speech and movement that is extremely artificial and, at the same time, more natural in impression than life itself. In this connexion the impact of the producer on the cast can be most effective.

Characters have to be portrayed. Not only each word, but also each movement, each mannerism, each gesture, helps the player to play a part. But a characteristic movement, essential to truthful portrayal, can, if it is not harmonized with all the other effects that must be obtained for completeness, be irritating, embarrassing, and false when noted by the audience. The producer must be watchful in the player's interest, for a player can acquire bad stage habits unless he or she is on guard against their intrusion. During rehearsal these can be checked by the producer who thinks in terms of the presentation as a whole, while the player must primarily, but not exclusively, think of his or her contribution to it. "The motionless pose of John Gielgud in the second scene of *Hamlet* achieved a powerful expression of scorn, unwilling obedience, and pent up emotions," writes E. C. White[1] of one of this great actor's appearances. "Words could not have revealed greater bitterness or distaste than did this silent, immobile figure."

Worthy of reiteration is the point that a player's exceptional physical characteristics can be turned to professional advantage, if suitable opportunities for their employment can be created or discovered opportunely. None the less, they restrict scope; they can be the cause of exclusion from a cast. To develop this line of thought can easily concentrate attention on abnormalities that press their possessors into an awkwardly circumscribed category. They are not specially in mind here.

An adolescent who thinks of a stage career will, acting wisely, have undertaken a course of training for professional work at, say, The Guildhall School of Music and Drama, The Royal Academy of Dramatic Art, or other reputable training institution, following, perhaps, consideration of various replies that are returned to the question "Can Acting Be Taught?"

Active association with amateur work during the early stages of interest in a stage career can be of practical value. Some amateur societies have professional producers. Their methods, closely observed and responded to during rehearsal, are helpful. So, too, is the work that has to be done behind the scenes. Stage management, organization of the details that are essential for the appropriate dressing and mounting of a play, expert guidance in make-up—these are both interesting and useful facets of stagework that have given amateurs an understanding of the exacting requirements of the professional stage.

[1] *Problems of Acting and Play Production.*

When aptitude and ability gain recognition by securing their possessor a part in a professional production, there may at first be slight chances to demonstrate exceptional gifts, or even average talent, but even the smallest part can be made to serve as a stepping-stone. How it is played is conditioned by the producer's domination and direction. An imaginative player with a sense of the stage and a clear conception of the relationship of small part to the other more important and pivotal parts, may be permitted to be more creative than are the leading members of the cast—but only if his part is made to dovetail into the complex whole.

Team Work

The producer, noting good work that is done by a player whose chances to demonstrate scope and range are rigorously limited, can be influential in advancing the player in his or her career. Knowing his responsibility, he will be as exacting in obtaining good work from the small-part players as he must be in ensuring that the players who fill the principal roles meet, as far as is practicable, his requirements. He must be a person of authority: he *is* in authority and must see not only each member of a cast but also a team. His eyes are the eyes of the members of the audience—with a difference. Theatregoers who see his production are in search of entertainment. He himself must do his best to see that it is provided, but while the average theatregoer will not understand how results are obtained, how points are registered, how effects are secured, the producer, knowing thoroughly the alphabet of acting, will bring into play the techniques that make meaningful and pointed whatever happens to be the content of the script. His work begins when he reads it imaginatively and with understanding, and ends when the curtain goes up on the first night's performance, after which only minor modifications and occasional re-vitalizing of interpretations and portrayals should be necessary.

Each player's work starts seriously when, probably as the result of an audition, perhaps by fortunate circumstances that do not arise out of superior talent discovered by competitive methods, his part on paper is made available for study. Much of what takes place at rehearsals, whatever dictation is given by the producer and submitted to by the players, is the outcome of co-operative work. A vivacious actress, a volatile actor, may be brilliant as an individual player, but brilliance may be the opposite of what is wanted as an individual member of a team. The producer's task is to dim the brilliance without destroying the life that should be inherent in portrayal and interpretation. Forbes Robertson, Sir Frank Benson, Beerbohm Tree, Irving, and others may have outshone the players who were associated with them; today there may be actors in the line of succession who prefer to have as members of the same cast inferior players so that by contrast the better is made to appear better still. The ideal is for any cast to be composed of players each of whom when chosen was the best for his or her part in the opinion of an expert whose judgment was based on the recognition of essentials for theatrical effectiveness and the attainment of aesthetic standards.

One most successful actor, John Gielgud, possessing an exceptional sense of the artistic significance of team-work, writing autobiographically made these points:[1] ". . . it is not easy to describe how actors go about their business. Perhaps, too, it is more seemly that these mysteries should remain a secret. No one can understand the technical side of the theatre until he himself comes to practise it. . . . But the struggles and agonies of the actor, as he winds his way through his labyrinthine process every night upon the stage, are of very little account or interest to anyone except himself. No one cares or is aware that he works for many months to correct some physical trick, or fights against his vocal mannerisms, or experiments with pauses, emphasis, timing, processes of thought. No one knows if he is suffering in his heart while he plays an emotional scene, or if he is merely adding up his household bills, considering what he will order for dinner, or regretting what he ate for lunch. Last night's audience, which he cursed for its unresponsiveness, may have enjoyed his performance every whit as much as to-night's, with which he feels the most cordial and personal sympathy."

These reflections are personal but not quite right. The

[1] *Early Stages.*

struggles and agonies of the actor can be of great account and of unusual interest to the critic in the theatre. He has to be alert to every influence that emanates from the stage. He has to see, to hear, to understand what is going on, what the players try to do, and how they do it or fail. He has to hear what the player says and to see what each player does. He has to convince himself, or confess failure, that he knows why certain things are done, and why the human voice is used on words, phrases, and lines to produce effects that are registered by members of the audience, even though he himself may be indifferent, phlegmatic, unimpressed, non-responsive. He may agree that the player who takes up, deliberately and yet with-out making the audience aware that his movement is deliberate, a position at a specific point during the performance does so for artistic reasons. He may note that a player has tricks and mannerisms which sometimes point lines and emphasize the significance of situations but which, on balance, militate against ease and smoothness, considering the performance as a whole. He may think the stage is too crowded or too bare; that the crowd, as in the 1950 performance of *Julius Caesar* at the Memorial Theatre, Stratford-on-Avon, is too virile and overpowering so that it makes a bad impression on the audience, the members of which, again as at the *Julius Caesar* performance, may have difficulty in hearing what the principals contribute to the development of the story of the play.

The critic in the theatre may, throughout a performance, remain unperturbed by action that is, or that should be, intended to intensify interest. He may decide that the story of the play is adequate, but that the players whose job it is to tell it by their acting and interpretation are unsuitable or that they fail to make the most of themselves and of their oppor-tunities. Conversely, he may be agreeably astonished that such a weak, or conventional, or dull play can be made dynamic and virile by players whose technique and talent are superbly harnessed to yield striking and effective artistic and other results.

The variants of what the critic in the theatre may note are many. At the end of any performance, whatever his opinions are, he has to decide for himself to what extent the producer has shaped the players, how each player has employed talent, ability, and gifts as an individual player, and also as a player whose contribution to the whole has had to be made in relation to other players.

The critic in the theatre seldom knows for certain whether when he notes what he thinks are weaknesses, misinterpretations, underplayiı g or overplaying, he should blame the producer for failing to mould his players to the design and shape of the production, or the players for failure to act in accordance with expert direction.

For the measurement of these aspects of production and performance the critic in the theatre has no standard measuring rod. Human beings are not machines—a trite remark that applies to producer, players, audience, and the critic in the theatre. There is abundance of scope for differences, for flexibility, for the human personality to reflect variants of itself in response to temperament, mood, and the circumstances of the moment. These are affected by health, by mental attitudes towards the immediate tasks in hand, by "the feeling of the house," i.e. the responsiveness or insensitivity of the audience as the performance proceeds. It is to be expected then that expert opinions on the public performance of a play given in a theatre will differ. Each different opinion can crystallize some of the truth, and also miss, overestimate, or undervalue basic points. When thinking in terms of production, of acting, of criticism, human, personal, and other elements have to be evaluated, and it is often exceedingly hard to discover, even when the impartial and judicial mind is in action, how these are poised, interwoven, and integrated in the public performance. Specialized knowledge and the ability to apply it are not a guarantee of irrefutable judgment. To allow a margin for human error that arises out of human frailties and foibles is permissible. Effects of the personal elements are not always readily discernible, or, when they are seen, convincingly explained.

The critic in the theatre proceeds warily (but does not permit himself to overthrow his own standards) with the affirmation of his opinions on points on which the producer may have been dogmatic and certain of his absolute rightness, or on which a player may be but reflecting complete obedience to direction. If blame for blemishes must be apportioned, perhaps the producer should be dealt with most severely, for he is the man (or woman) in charge. He is there to produce, and if he cannot get what he wants from one set of players, there are always other players available, which is not the same as contending that they can, in practical life, be invited to supersede the unsatisfactory players!

From whatever angle production and performance are appraised there will be extenuating circumstances upon which to draw for explanations of departures from perfection or any particularly high standard of achievement that has been fixed as the ideal. Among these are personal elements which are never wholly under the absolute control of any one individual, even the individual from whom they emanate.

CHAPTER VII

THE CRITIC'S STANDARDS

IMPERSONAL elements, which are also integral to production, performance, and audience reaction, must, on first thoughts, be considered to be as important as the personal elements that are indivisible from personal expressions. Reflection may seriously disturb what first thoughts create. Actually, there is no necessity for the critic in the theatre to accept, at one outset, any particular scale of relative values. All values that are inherent in the production and performance of a play in the theatre are important, and the critic cannot safely ignore them. It is not even advisable to say that many of them are more directly concerned with the traffic of the stage, the commerce of the theatre, than with the aesthetics of production and the art of acting.

Mounting, dressing, lighting, theatrical effects—these are auxiliary aids to the creation of theatrical illusion. They impinge upon applied production principles and the employment of technique in the art of acting.

It is equally inadvisable for producer, players, or the critic in the theatre to assume that members of the audience will be unaware of blemishes, anachronisms, falsities, attempts to fob them off with the unsuitable, the meretricious, or the expedient. The average theatregoer will not always be aware of the great care that may have been exercised in order to ensure, for example, avoidance of anachronistic furnishing. It would be unreasonable to expect him or her to recognize at a glance the appropriateness of a chair, or a table, or a cabinet, or other piece of furniture that only study and research —or special knowledge—have proved to be the right piece to include in the mounting of a period play. And it would be unsafe to assume that an effect will not be ruined if producer or player has managed to produce the wrong effect in the right place!

It is unlikely that the critic in the theatre will have knowledge so extensive and so highly specialized that he is able to check at sight and away from his reference library the authenticity of everything that is introduced into the mounting of a play, the costuming of it, or even the lighting of it. It is not essential that he should have such knowledge, and, fundamentally, it is not essential that every detail of a production and performance should be historically true or scientifically exact. The primary aim is to create illusion, or to propagate ideas, or to provide entertainment that may have little to do with truth to life. Towards the attainment of this aim convention has imposed conventional requirements, but these change from age to age and from country to country.

Although the Greeks and the Elizabethans represented life in action on the stage, their representations were different from ours. Greek tragedy, for example, concentrates on the reflection and illumination of human psychology; Elizabethan drama on character. They worked from the inside outwards. Action was not necessarily the mainspring of character-portrayal. The Greeks were interested in what people think and feel, and in how thoughts and feelings, dynamic and expressive, affect human beings. Character is not the exclusive and primary interest of the Elizabethans, but their successors, the Restorationists, and the Moderns more frequently than did the Elizabethans, eschew fundamental or universal characterization; debase and depreciate character by admitting the superficial and in a measure the extraneous. Neither Greek nor Latin literature yields an appreciable volume of writing that deals specially with dramatic theory.

When the commercial—or any other—theatre turns to Greek drama for production and performance there is now an abundance of reference material, as there is when the desire is to produce and to perform Elizabethan or Restoration plays. The producer who has to handle a contemporary play is most unlikely to be at a loss to discover sources of practical guidance.

These considerations arise when expert angles of the traffic of the stage are under review.

The average theatregoer, principally through ignorance that is not mentioned in any derogatory sense or through lack

of effective power, must accept what is offered. The critic in
the theatre is made a like offering, but he is not expected to be
so ready in acceptance. The average theatregoer who goes
to the theatre for simple, straightforward entertainment is not
keenly interested in what the expert critic in the theatre
writes about the particular entertainment, although he may
turn to read a newspaper report of it. "I wonder what *he* will
say about it?" is the commonplace query of the theatregoer
who is more than superficially interested in plays and their
performance. When he, the critic, writes he is conscious of the
fact that his opinions will be noted by some enthusiasts. He is
also conscientious, and, therefore, desirous of writing with
authority. This desire impels him to probe beneath the surface
of production and performance, to be analytical, and, as a
result, on occasions to be justly condemnatory or justifiably
appreciative.

There will be numerous opportunities for diversity of
genuine views. Take the setting of a play. It can be of great
importance, but it can be relatively so inconsequential that
authenticity is of secondary importance. This is a dangerous
attitude of mind to adopt towards evaluation. At the same
time, it is possible to be so academic and pedantic as to devalue
production and performance for slender reasons.

The performance, through production, is the picture.
Certainly the frame, the setting, by being worthy of the
picture, can enhance the attractiveness of it. Accuracy in
both letter and spirit will, in some cases, be essential, but in
many plays that are written for their popular theatrical
entertainment values, the frame can be any one of a number
of frames, and there can be interesting, challenging, imitative
variations of the one frame that is accepted as being the best
for its specific purpose.

I am reminded of the setting for *Hamlet*. Act I, Sc. 1 is
"Elsinore. A Platform before the Castle." For subsequent
scenes there are "A Room of State in the Castle," "A Room in
Polonius' House," "A Hall in the Castle," and variants.
When columnist and essayist Ian Mackay toured the Scan-
dinavian countries in 1950, and found himself in Denmark he
"walked out of Kronborg Castle, on to the famous platform

at Elsinore." His visit prompted him to write a special article entitled "Ghosts Don't Walk in Daylight." Here is something of what he wrote in the *News Chronicle*: "Being a Highlandman, however, and therefore scared of ghosts, even when they are royal ones, I turned up at noon and not, as young Hamlet did, at midnight. . . . At first sight, despite the clean, crisp sparkling sunlight, the string of taxis at the end of the drawbridge and the racket of the electric riveters in the nearby shipyard, the place seemed very much as it was when Hamlet called upon angels and ministers of grace to defend him, and Marcellus muttered there was something rotten in the state of Denmark.

"No cock crowed or ghost came, it is true, and the nearest thing to hell itself breathing out was when a provocative little man in the manner of the Skibbereen Eagle informed me that he had his eye on Russia.

"But Francisco was there upon his watch waiting for Bernardo to relieve him, only this time instead of casque and cuirasse he wore British battle-dress and carried a tommy-gun instead of a pike.

"There, however, the likeness ceased. For the rest I regret to report that Shakespeare was a bad reporter. He wouldn't last a week on the Press Association. His Elsinore is as much like the real place as the Grand Canyon is like the Norfolk Broads. . . .

"It is usually Horatio who gets things wrong. Take that business of the beetling cliff, for instance. When Hamlet follows the ghost, Horatio—just as Dr. Watson used to do to Holmes—implored him to be careful.

" 'What if he tempt you toward the flood, my lord,' he cries, 'or to the dreadful summit of the cliff that beetles o'er his base into the sea?' Then to make sure Hamlet knew what was coming to him he goes on: 'The very place puts toys of desperation without more motive into every brain that looks so many fathoms to the sea and hears it roar beneath.'

"It almost gives you vertigo to read it. But the fact is there is no cliff, or dreadful summit within miles of Elsinore and the number of fathoms to the sea is exactly nil. When I was there the kids were jumping from the platform to the shore.

"Hamlet would have been in much greater danger on the platform of a Number 11 bus.

"I am not so sure about Ophelia's brook, but here again I'll bet it is in Warwickshire. All I saw in the way of inland water was a greasy canal with a Peek Frean biscuit tin floating on it.

"The truth is that Shakespeare's *Hamlet* has no more to do with Denmark than *King Lear* has to do with Kent. Most of the characters have Roman names, except for a few minor hangers-on like Osric the 'waterfly,' Rosencrantz and Guildenstern and the clowns in the churchyard who, of course, come straight from Stratford-on-Avon.

"In fact, that platform in *Hamlet* might just as well have been placed in Palermo or Pernambuco. It bears a remarkable resemblance to the battlements at Inverness and every time I hear that cock crow at the Old Vic I feel he is answering the owl in *Macbeth*.

"For *Hamlet* is not a territorial tragedy. It is part of the texture of eternity and the scene might as well be laid in Market Harborough or Mars for all it matters."

The Play's Setting

I have quoted Ian Mackay's lightly-brightly-pertinently written article because of its point. A playwright may give his play a sternly realistic setting, or, taking imaginative flight, exercise to the full the licence that is granted to poets and other creative literary artists. The producer of T. S. Eliot's *The Cocktail Party* is provided with the poet-playwright's settings. They are:

Act One. Scene 1. The drawing-room of the Chamberlaynes' London flat. Early evening.
Scene 2. The same room: a quarter of an hour later.
Scene 3. The same room: late afternoon of the next day.
Act Two. Sir Henry Harcourt-Reilly's consulting room in London: several weeks later.
Act Three. The drawing-room of the Chamberlaynes' London flat. Two years later. A late afternoon in July.

This can be transferred from page to stage in more than one way, but there is less scope for imaginative treatment than

there is with the setting of, say, the second act of Bernard
Shaw's "Comedy of No Manners" *Buoyant Billions*, which
I saw at the 1949 (and last) Malvern Festival, and, again,
shortly afterwards at the Princes Theatre, London. The
scene is:

> A Jungle Clearing in Panama.

When the average theatregoer is "translated to the depths
of the wood in the enchantment of a moonlit night" (Barrie's
phraseology) at the opening of the second act of *Dear Brutus*,
imaginative treatment will no doubt make a stronger visual
appeal to him than the orthodox setting that Priestley's
Laburnum Grove is likely to make:

> The whole action takes place in the living room of the Redferns'
> house, *Ferndale*, Laburnum Grove, Shooters Green, a suburb of
> North London.

Few theatregoers, if asked to visualize such a room, would
fail to get approximately near to acceptable description.

The Restorationists were neither fastidious nor detailed.
In The Mermaid Series Sir John Vanbrugh's *The Relapse* has
for the opening scene

> Scene 1.—Enter Loveless, reading.

with a footnote by the editor, A. E. H. Swain, "Leigh Hunt
added several stage directions. I have throughout retained
those given in the edition of 1776, merely numbering the scenes
for convenience sake. In this case Hunt adds: 'A Room in
Loveless's *Country House*'."

This is less exacting than Sean O'Casey's setting of the
second act of his tragi-comedy in four acts (*The Silver Tassie*).
It is:

> "In the war zone: a scene of jagged and lacerated ruin of
> what was once a monastery. At back a lost wall and window are
> indicated by an arched piece of broken coping pointing from the
> left to the right, and a similar piece of masonry pointing from
> the right to the left. Between these two lacerated fingers of stone
> can be seen the country stretching to the horizon where the
> front trenches are. Here and there heaps of rubbish mark where
> houses once stood. From some of these lead, dead hands are
> protruding. Further on spiky stumps of trees which were once
> a small wood. The ground is dotted with rayed and shattered
> shell holes. Across the horizon in the red glare can be seen the

criss-cross pattern of the barbed wire bordering the trenches. In the sky sometimes a green star, sometimes a white star, burns. Within the broken archway to the left is an arched entrance to another part of the monastery, used now as a Red Cross Station. In the wall, right, near the front is a stained-glass window, background green, figure of the Virgin, white-faced, wearing a black robe, lights inside making the figure vividly apparent. Further up from this window is a life-size crucifix. A shell has released an arm from the cross, which has caused the upper part of the figure to lean forward with the released arm outstretched towards the figure of the Virgin. Underneath the crucifix on a pedestal, in red letters, are the words: Princeps Pacis. Almost opposite the crucifix is a gunwheel to which Barney is tied. At the back, in the centre, where the span of the arch should be, is the shape of a big howitzer gun, squat, heavy underpart, with a long, sinister barrel now pointing towards the front at an angle of forty-five degrees. At the base of the gun a piece of wood is placed on which is chalked, Hyde Park Corner. On another piece of wood near the entrance of the Red Cross Station is chalked, No Hawkers or Street Cries Permitted Here. In the near centre is a brazier in which a fire is burning. Crouching near the fire is a soldier whose clothes are covered with mud and splashed with blood. Every feature of the scene seems a little distorted from its original appearance. Rain is falling steadily; its fall worried now and again by fitful gusts of a cold wind. A small organ is heard playing slow and stately notes as the curtain rises.

Examples could be multiplied. The playwright "sets" his play, and his setting must, or should, be considered. Actually, it should be seriously considered and in richness of detail for the attainment of the aim of production and performance, i.e. the theatrical presentation and interpretation of the author's intention.

My citations from Restoration drama and modern drama are intentional. I heard one producer of *Love for Love* stop an actress's attempt at interpretation by telling her, before giving her instructional guidance, that she was supposed to be playing a Restoration comedy but was giving the impression that she was trying to be an Elizabethan actress—style in acting changes as does style in playwriting and production— hence my reference to *The Silver Tassie*, parts of which by the style of writing call for and receive expressionistic production. A reasonable certainty about the setting of a play is that in the opinion of those who are responsible it will aid production and performance.

I have referred to "setting," which is the starting-point of integrated parts. With "setting" there is "mounting"—the two are often used as synonyms. There are, however, differences. I will give another purposive example, Aldous Huxley's *The Gioconda Smile*. The first scene is—

> The living-room of Henry Hutton's house in the Thames Valley, not far from Windsor.

This is sufficiently indicative for the producer to make a beginning. When the playwright proceeds to give descriptive details of the "mounting," the producer who would strive at all costs after verisimilitude would be confronted with obstacles or would make attempts that really need not be made in order to create an environment that is in harmony with the author's intentions. The time is—

> Summer in the early 'thirties.

The details are—

> The room is characteristically "modern" in design. One wall consists entirely of plate-glass windows, which give on to a paved veranda, beyond which is the garden. Seen from the audience's viewpoint, this wall of glass slants diagonally from left to right, forming an angle, at about the centre of the stage, with one of the interior walls of the room. This means that a considerable portion of the stage remains outside the glass, so that it is possible for action to proceed on the veranda while still being visible to the audience. There is a door in the back wall and another, of glass, giving on to the veranda. In warm weather it is possible to roll back the sheets of glass, so that the room is almost completely open on the garden side. Pictures by well-known French artists, such as Matisse, Bracque, Leger, Modigliani, hang on the back wall. The room is furnished in the style predominating at the Paris Exposition of Decorative Arts in 1926. A small table is spread for lunch. Hutton sits facing the audience, with Janet Spence on his right. Opposite Janet is the place, momentarily unoccupied, of Nurse Braddock. Hutton is a man of forty-five, handsome, full of charm, a good talker. Janet is about ten years younger, very well bred, very much a lady, but too intense in manner to be a very comfortable companion. As the scene opens, Clara, the parlourmaid, is clearing away the first course and setting out the dessert plates. Hutton picks up the decanter and turns to Janet.

If any producer endeavoured to mount this particular scene without departing in details from the author's description, he would introduce with his exactitude unnecessary works of art at risks that would not be worth running, and without attaining higher artistic and aesthetic standards than would be attained by the judicious exercise of imagination. Moreover, the average theatregoer would be as satisfied with the "paintings" that suggested works of art by any of the masters as by seeing the works themselves. Indeed, and paradoxically, the "inferior" in this context may easily be the "superior."

The producer's imagination in action is a great asset. The mounting of a play such as Priestley's *They Came To A City* can heighten the tension that is created by the play's action. The theatregoers who see this particular play in performance never see the city represented, but their interest in what sort of a city it is is intensified by the mounting, plus other factors in production such as the movements of the players, their facial expression, their gestures, their "lines" when they reappear after visiting the city.

Glaring anachronisms in mounting, if permitted, would be noted by the average theatregoer: for example, a modern typewriter, a telephone, a dictaphone, introduced into a play written today but purporting to be about human life in former centuries, say, Clifford Bax's romantic *A Rose Without a Thorn*, which deals with Queen Elizabeth and her times. Falsities, pieces of furniture of the wrong periods, say, would probably go unnoticed, but blemishes could easily be caused by placing tables, chairs, desks, etc., in positions that impeded the appropriate and significant movement of players and could just as easily create annoyance.

These, again, are indicative rather than exhaustive remarks, and are mentioned merely to refer to points which the critic in the theatre notes, perhaps sometimes with exasperation, and which the average theatregoer may fail to note without any sacrifice of entertainment values.

Period Costuming

Similar remarks apply to dressing or costuming.

Charles B. Cochran in his Foreword, written during the

height of his theatrical activities, to Nevil Truman's valuable
guide to period costumes[1] furnished supporting evidence: "I
would venture to suggest that, for stage purposes, there are
few instances of plays in which the very strictest historical
accuracy is necessary. While I am always anxious to create
on the stage the right atmosphere of period for an audience,
this can often be done better by a slight departure from
exactitude. An audience, seeing a play, will not have Mr.
Nevil Truman's knowledge of costume; it will, at best, have a
rough and ready idea of 'the sort of thing' that people wore at
different epochs. Sometimes it may be better to indulge the
popular conception, even if it is not accurate.

"We may have a play about a historical event of which we
know the exact date. Here, except in the case of leading
personages with whose appearance and dress the man in the
street is familiar through pictures, I would willingly allow my
designer the rope of ten years either way, earlier or later. It
might happen that the exactly right fashion was an extra-
ordinarily ugly one from the point of view of the stage pictures,
or inconvenient for the actors, whereas a few years previously
or subsequently the style of dress was better for the producer's
purpose. As long as the general spirit and atmosphere of the
time are created, and the stage effect is pleasing, the demands
of the theatre are satisfied."

A hint taken from these two authorities is that the correct
costuming of a play involves entry into a highly specialized
and intensely fascinating world, but that the journey is not
really necessary in order to give the average theatregoer
satisfaction through the presentation of period plays. This
non-essential of play production and performance should not,
however, stifle intellectual curiosity at the outset and stultify
research, which, undertaken, would enable the correct answers
to be returned to such questions as: In which order should
ecclesiastical costume be worn? (This is, perhaps, more often
wrongly worn on the stage than any other type.) What are
the principal styles of armour (style needed for open-air
pageantry, period plays, etc.)? How were the Dandies of the
nineteenth century dressed? When and how was the crinoline

[1] *Historic Costuming.*

made and worn? During which century were the Spanish cape, the Italian doublet, and the Venetian trunkhose fashionable?

Style of acting is affected by the style of clothes that is imposed upon the players by the period of the play. One generalization is that professional actors and actresses know how to wear costume and how to act in it. Occasionally, however, one notices a member of a cast whose appearance suggests a dummy in costume rather than a human being wearing costume with the naturalness with which non-theatrical clothing is worn, and in some amateur societies the players create laughter on their first appearance because they look neither natural nor comfortable in their period costumes.

Lighting

Lighting is another impersonal element which the producer must use with discretionary effectiveness, especially in these modern days when electricity in the theatre can be more of a specialized toy than a scientific aid that is at the service of the expert-artist-specialist.

Time has marched rapidly onward since R. D'Oyly Carte, in October, 1881, in an inaugural address in which he dealt with "the manifold pomps and glories" of the new Savoy, said:[1] "From the time, now some years since, that the first electric lights in lamps were exhibited outside the Paris Opera-house, I have been convinced that electric light in some form is the light of the future for use in theatres, not to go further. The peculiar steely blue colour and the flicker which are inevitable in all systems of 'arc' lights, however, make them unsuitable for use in any but very large buildings. The invention of the 'incandescent lamp' has now paved the way for the application of electricity to lighting houses, and consequently theatres. . . . There are several extremely good incandescent lamps, but I finally decided to adopt that of Mr. J. W. Swan, the well-known inventor, of Newcastle-on-Tyne. The enterprise of Messrs. Siemens Bros. & Co. has enabled me to try the experiment of exhibiting this light in my theatre. About 1,200 lights are used, and the power to generate

[1] *Gilbert, Sullivan and D'Oyly Carte.*

a sufficient current for these is obtained from large steam-engines, giving about 120 horse-power, placed on some open land near the theatre. The new light is not only used in the audience part of the theatre, but on the stage, for footlights, side and top lights, etc., and (not of the least importance for the comfort of the performers) in the dressing-rooms—in fact, in every part of the house. This is the first time that it has been attempted to light any public building entirely by electricity. What is being done is an experiment, and may succeed or fail. It is not possible . . . to guarantee absolutely against any break-down of the electric light. To provide against such a contingency gas is laid on through the building, and the 'pilot' light on the central sunburner will always be kept alight, so that in case of accident the theatre can be flooded with gas-light in a few seconds. . . . If the experiment of electric lighting succeeds, there can be no question of the enormous advantages to be gained in purity of air and coolness—advantages the value of which it is hardly possible to over-estimate."

Half a century later Herbert M. Prentice, closely associated with the Sheffield and Birmingham repertory and other theatres for some years, introducing what was, at the time, the latest authoritative words on stage lighting by two of its foremost exponents, C. Harold Ridge and F. S. Aldred, wrote: "Stage lighting is not a firework display—nor should the result be stage-darkening. Colour has a significance of its own. It can interpret the spirit of the play and create the right atmosphere, but it must not obtrude and throw out the balance of harmony."

Later still, and again furnishing up-to-date and authoritative writing on the subject, Robert Nesbitt, introducing Frederick Bentham's book[1] pointed out: "The history of stage lighting is the story of development from the primitive to the complex; of the harnessing of scientific knowledge to theatrical purposes. The modern trend, most significantly, is away from the overall lighting provided by magazine battens and lengths." Mr. Bentham himself opened his exposition: "Stage lighting must always be considered as part of the show, sometimes a small

---

[1] *Stage Lighting.*

part, purely subservient to the actor or the scenery, but at other times dominant and even overriding the actor."

Mr. P. Corry suggests in his imaginative and constructive book[1] that "he who devises the lighting in terms of direction, intensity, and colour should be known as a lighting designer," and concludes: "The producer must always see the play as a whole and be for ever striving to attain theatrical significance. In the attainment of that significance he must have light, that the audience may see; and he must constantly seek those subtleties of shade that will make perception acute."

One catchphrase, often repeated, is: "The play's the thing"— yes, when its text, scenery, dressing, acting, make-up, lighting, stage effects, etc., are handled as parts to be brought together in a harmonious composite whole. The producer will not be at a loss to know which principles of lighting to apply when the playwright indicates that a scene has to be played in the open-air, in sunshine, at dusk, in a darkened room, etc. Lighting to give effect to these relatively straightforward requirements can be mishandled. More subtle, indirect, artistic, usage of modern stage lighting to create "atmosphere," to bring out the spirit of a love scene, an emotional scene, moments of suspense, and other significant passages in the progress of the performance of a play working towards its climax; also the skilful manipulation of lighting that is often a concomitant of "thrillers," plays of adventure and misadventure, are problems of production that must be solved by discussion among various specialists. Sometimes the solutions are sound theatrically, but inefficiency on the mechanical side destroys the illusion for the average theatregoer.

Then there are "behind the scenes" activities that have to be organized by the producer and carried out by experienced workers who play important, if unseen, parts.

Arnold Ridley, who had done much successful playwriting and acting before his name was sent round the world by the successful production of *The Ghost Train*, which on its West-End production at St. Martin's in November, 1925, began to be talked about in a new way, largely because of the train effects, has written interestingly on this subject. E. Holman Clarke,

[1] *Lighting the Stage*

the producer, Mr. Ridley has pointed out,[1] immediately "established illusion on the stage. The play opened by the curtain rising on a set that depicted an ordinary country station waiting-room. Every detail was correct—a smoky lamp, cracked and dim; an untended fire burning in a dirty grate; a floor covered with orange peel; empty cigarette packets and stub-ends; casual litter; the water bottle with a broken glass; steamy windows; bills advertising out-of-date excursions, and orders restricting the movement of cattle during foot and mouth disease plagues. There was even framed advice to friendless girls arriving at the station. Such perfect detail had the effect upon the audience of making them say 'Ah, we are in a waiting room, presently we shall hear a train coming. Here it is! Splendid! Wonderful!' The effect itself was perfectly simple, being merely a judicious mixture of thunder sheets, compressed air, a garden roller, and pieces of sandpaper and wire brushes combined with a kettle-drum. There was nothing in fact that is out of reach of the smallest amateur society. But would that train *suggestion* off have been really effective without the perfect railway *illusion* on? Definitely not."

Thunder, rain, wind, snow, sea, lightning, fires, explosions— these are some of the effects that have been known to theatre-goers for a long time. Scientific inventions have added appreciably to them—the aeroplane, the motor-cycle, wireless, television, etc. Effectiveness in use is realized not only by discovering the best methods of producing them, but also by precision-timing, which can, in some situations, be of first-class importance. The revolver that will not make the desired noise at the right moment; the electric light that is switched on a few seconds too early or too late; the telephone bell that rings too soon or continues to ring when it should have stopped ringing; doors and windows that will not open; these are some of the noises and effects which, when not timed precisely, cause titters and laughs to spread throughout a theatre audience.

The critic in the theatre knows how easily some of the seemingly simplest mechanical devices that are designed to aid production and performance can fail to fulfil their purposes as

[1] *Theatre and Stage.*

and just when required. They provide him with additional chances to specify deficiencies in production and performance— and also any reasonable-minded commentator with the opportunity to contend that very much too much can be made of faults in these mechanistic aids to the presentation and interpretation of the playwright's intention.

Refinements in production can, in certain circumstances, reduce theatrical performances to the level at which the average theatregoer need not trouble to exercise his imagination. Film direction has made cinema-goers mentally lethargic because they have been persistently given all possible details in pictorial form, leaving them little scope for imaginative interpretation and deduction. In this connexion the living theatre is different, and, in the opinion of experts and entertainment-seekers alike, superior. Nevertheless, the impersonal elements that have been touched upon rather than treated exhaustively in this chapter are two-edged. They can, undoubtedly, be made to serve many and varied auxiliary purposes. In some cases they are indispensable and must be introduced. Their indispensability, however, does not mean that aesthetic considerations should be given only an insignificant or subordinate place.

The producer must weave these impersonal elements and the personal elements which spring from his direction and manipulation of human beings into a composite whole. The critic in the theatre must be able to unweave and to re-weave these without destroying the pattern and design imposed upon the performance as a whole by the producer, who is responsible for seeking the correct and appropriate interpretation of the playwright's intention through the medium of the team of which he is master.

CHAPTER VIII

THE CRITIC'S SYMPATHY

IT is one thing to attract theatregoers to support a theatrical performance; another, once they are inside the theatre, to create and to hold their interest by the provision of entertainment that fully meets their, perhaps, undefined expectations, and gives them satisfaction. Advertising and publicity methods are different today from what they were at the turn of the century, but the differences do not show an advance that has caught up with, much less surpassed, the sensational and the spurious superlatives that are in regular currency to induce theatregoers to support the cinema.

It is true that the playwright may express himself creatively without primary thought of the public performance of his play, but the great probability is that in the majority of cases writers of plays write them in the hope that they will be produced with a sensitiveness and appropriateness that will reveal and make clear their intention and be performed regularly throughout a period, preferably a long period, to the delight and satisfaction of theatregoers.

Now and again there are figures in the literary world that try, and fail, to write plays. Their grasp of language is firm, their knowledge is adequate, they are rich in ideas, they do not lack awareness of the World and of what constitutes Life for some human beings who live in it, but they are without the imagination, the flair, the knack to think or to write in terms of the theatre. Their "closet" drama remains in typescript and within the boards of books without the slightest chance that any producer, given the chance, could bring it to life in the theatre, and in this context bringing a play to life means transferring it as a living, virile entity from the stage to the members of the theatre audience. These may number scores, or hundreds—thousands in some of the totalitarian countries where open-air theatres were (and are) the form in which government demands and wishes are propagated and popularized. Their imaginations can be stimulated, their minds fed, their emotions played upon, their knowledge extended, their desire for pleasure met—but only when the performance catches and holds their attention and creates their pleasurable interest for a number of reasons that baffle comprehensive definition.

Writers of literary drama cannot reasonably hope to meet with commercial success in the theatre, but they often demonstrate talent and ability which, it is deducible in advance, are more than adequate to ensure successful authorship through published books. Their inability to turn themselves into popular playwrights is rooted in their incapacity as writers to express themselves in the form of a play so that when its content is worked upon by producer and players it makes a diversified appeal to theatregoers. On the other hand, playwrights of the theatre, in contradistinction to the literary playwrights of the study, have a theatrical sense. Their ideas and thoughts, their impression and reflections of the lives of human beings, are expressed so that they can be communicated convincingly from the stage. They are aware of the technical requirements of playwriting for the people and facile in meeting them—when they are successful. The success is never a foregone certainty.

Types of Theatregoer

A theatre audience is a conglomeration of people whose motives are mixed, whose moods function on different planes, whose emotions are stirred but not in all cases by the same stimuli.

One type of theatregoer is instantaneously "captured" by an impressive stage spectacle; another type by a series of "manufactured thrills" that register their effects at once, although on reflection the theatregoer, in calmer mood, acknowledges that he was "carried away" by momentary illusion or the distortion of fact which, at the time, struck a convincing note. Another type is satisfied if the idea content of a play meets the intellectual demands which he makes of the theatre. For him the play of ideas, even when it is written by a playwright who fails to blend iconoclastic dialogue and brilliant wit with theatrical effectiveness in the manner of Shaw, has a much stronger appeal than any murder or mystery story told in play form, no matter with what degree of technical skill. Another type is uncontrollably responsive emotionally when the playwright, through expert craftsmanship, and the producer, with superb stagecraft, arouse sympathy in the right ways which for this type may be making sentiment turn to sentimentality, dramatizing the romantic, intensifying the dramatic. Another type is phlegmatic and unmoved by impersonal elements in a stage performance, even when they are relevant and essential, but is suddenly brought to sentient life by what are considered to be flashes of universal truths that occur, perhaps unexpectedly, in the tense dialogue of strong personalities in a scene that portrays a battle of wits.

Both the playwright who writes deliberately for theatrical production and the producer who aims to satisfy his variegated audience by organizing the personal and the impersonal elements in a public performance are keenly aware of the varied demands that they must meet; also of the near impossibility of any one type of theatrical entertainment being made to suit the differing demands and varied tastes of all theatregoers.

Theatregoers include highbrows, middlebrows, and lowbrows; those who like theatrical spectacles; those who prefer modern comedies; those who make Shakespeare their theatrical giant; those who go to the theatre to see only revivals of what they have decided are plays of significance; those who support the theatre when they are convinced that what they will see will be entertainment that will fortify them in their prejudices or strengthen them in their convictions. Again, the classifications are capable of appreciable extension.

Elmer Rice, author of *Street Scene* and *Imperial City*, in his novel of theatrical life[1] gives an impression of one of his characters in observant mood: "From time to time Eric looked out at the spectators in the front rows, watching their expressive faces, their changes of mood and variations in attentiveness. It was a vivid demonstration of the power of the stage to rouse the emotions and to create an all-absorbing illusion. Momentarily, at least, this heterogeneous crowd was completely under

[1] *The Show Must Go On.*

the spell of a fiction produced by painted mimes, standing
before painted scenery, and speaking the lines he had written.
Though they knew it was all make-believe, the onlookers were
as profoundly moved as they would have been by reality,
perhaps considerably more moved, for the arts of the stage
gave shape and intensity to characters and events that, in
actuality, might seem prosaic and formless. As he stood there
in the darkness, hearing his words spoken, watching those
faces, and feeling the emotional impact of the invisible hundreds
in the theatre, Eric had the deep satisfaction of knowing that
his was the power to entrance, to stir, to exhilarate. Creation
was a lonely joy, and not without pain, but public appreciation
linked him to his fellow men and made him feel strong and
secure."

But not all theatregoers react in harmony; "drifters" whose
visit to the theatre is casual and non-selective can remain
unmoved, indifferent.

During 1950 a capital sum of £15,000 was found to make
possible the production of *The Trial*, a play based on the novel
of Franz Kafka and translated by Jacqueline and Frank
Sundstrom from a dramatization of the novel by André Gide
and Jean-Louis Barrault. There is always a risk in transferring
to the stage a piece of writing that was originally cast in another
form, a play from a novel, for instance, or the dramatization
of a short story, or even a biography of a V.I.P. It is a risk
that is run by both theatrical managements and cinema
managements. Sometimes transference enhances values, or,
in results, proves to have been an experiment well worth
making. Such, for example, was the stage presentation of
Dostoievsky's novel *Crime and Punishment* (163 performances),
with which were associated the names of Rodney Ackland,
Anthony Quayle, and John Gielgud. It is a matter of opinion
whether a similar remark can apply to the Kafka experiment.
If the theatregoers' answer can be accepted as conclusive it did
not justify itself, for the play had only six performances at the
Winter Garden. The critics in the theatre were, in general,
not in two minds about the production. Alan Dent in the
News Chronicle wrote "Franz Kafka's *The Trial* judged as a play
is a triumphant example of Supreme Bosh. There is nothing

in it. . . . I blame Messieurs Gide and Barrault more than anybody else, since the novel was quite obviously undramatisable in the very first place." His colleague, Beverley Baxter, M.P., in the *Evening Standard*, dealing with the production, wrote: "Any dramatist who tries to make a play out of a novel is faced with difficulties. But when a Swedish actor and his wife translate into English the French dramatisation of a novel by a Czech author the result is almost certain to be disastrous. . . . A large company of actors, some of them distinguished but many of them indistinct, laboured in rehearsal and hoped they were on a winner. When the gallery laughed ironically they still loyally played their parts with that discipline which is so fine a tradition in the theatre."

Sometimes the theatregoers in the gallery laugh; sometimes they boo, but sometimes they are wildly enthusiastic though not necessarily sharply critical. The laughing galleryites at the Kafka play were uninterested and not obvious "highbrows"— the heading given to Alan Dent's criticism was "Kafka on the Stage is Higher Bosh." Have war experiences since the opening of the twentieth century had any important influence on theatrical taste, in making clearer what the average theatregoer expects or wants? Have they increased the value and importance of drama and the theatre in contemporary life? After the Second World War people found themselves in an age of confusion, conflict, and complexity—a trite statement but also true and troublesome for those in pursuit of intellectual and spiritual tranquillity. But the post-Second World War years were (and are) different from those that many lived through after the 1914–18 War. Part of one recurring problem is how the average theatregoer will continue to react to the dramatic and theatrical entertainment that is provided.

I was reminded of this fact by the revival of Terence Rattigan's *French Without Tears*. When this light comedy was produced at the Criterion Theatre early in November, 1936, the professional appraisers were warmly appreciative and the theatregoing public avidly avaricious. It ran for two and a half years and made its author about £23,000—not an inconsiderable return for the imaginative-analytical-observational-expressive work involved in presenting, in play form, what was subsequently described as "a typical study of Bright Young Things in search of a mate, unhampered by parents or guardians."

Ernest Short, in 1942, wrote:[1] "Among the repercussions due to the flapper element in post-war audiences were the plays which showed that young women were in no mood to limit their choice of men friends to those whom parents judged desirable as home-makers. Aiding and abetting this revolt, and emphasizing its comedies and tragedies, came a batch of plays suggesting that a girl might be quite happy wedded to engineer, tradesman or stockbroker, whatever Papa or Mama think." *French Without Tears* was one of the plays in this batch.

In another post-war age the pre-war Rattigan light comedy of 1936 was revived. With what results? The keen edge of the dramatic critics' taste had been blunted, possibly by the harshnesses, the futilities, and the inanities of much of life and of living since those uncertain but relatively smooth days of '36, and playgoers saw in it a piece of history presented rather than realistically conceived.

When James Agate referred to Mr. Rattigan in one of his volumes, which are a record of the theatrical times in which he lived and expressed himself, he stated:[2] "Mr. Rattigan is the author of the most successful farce of modern times. Presumably it would have been easy for him to continue to provoke what Goldsmith so unkindly calls the loud laugh that speaks the vacant mind. But Mr. Rattigan's mind is by no means vacant. His present piece is largely a re-arrangement of old spots in a new pattern." Having gone into detail, he added: "Now I see nothing here that is not praiseworthy. Mr. Rattigan has at least perceived that people are not necessarily all of a piece."

A more recently published book also has a reference to Mr. Rattigan. This is what a playwright-dramatic-critic, W. A. Darlington, wrote in his final chapter, "The Theatre in Convalescence":[3] "It soon became clear that a playgoing population which was, or might at any moment be, in

---

[1] *Theatrical Cavalcade.*   [2] *The Amazing Theatre.*
[3] *The Actor and His Audience.*

immediate danger of death had an attitude to its playgoing quite different from that of a public opinion outside the area of acute danger; it was willing, and at times, eager, to face truth. Naturally, it had a liking for light, gay pieces, but it did not close its mind to serious or unhappy things as the London public of the former world war had insisted on doing, with a frenzied escapism that had lasted far into the 1920's and had helped to keep down the artistic standards of that unhappy period. Two plays may be used to illustrate this point." Mr. Darlington's second citation is Rattigan's *Flare Path*, produced at the Apollo Theatre in August, 1942. Of this Air Force play Mr. Darlington wrote that it was "light enough in texture but with an underlying seriousness of intention, giving a realistic picture of the life of carefully hidden anxiety and terror lived by the wives and sweethearts of the bomber crews. This was accepted by the public with even greater satisfaction than the other (Emlyn Williams's *The Morning Star*), for it ran for over six hundred and fifty performances. It is significant that when these plays reached New York, which was in the struggle yet outside the danger area, as London had been in the first war, and consequently was in the same obstinately escapist frame of mind, both were rejected out of hand on the ground that they were very bad plays."

Has emotion returned, or is it returning, to the theatre in this post-Second Great War period? Mr. Darlington thinks that: "One great hope for the future of our theatre is the fact that not only the audiences and the actors but the best of our practising dramatists now realize the paramount importance of the emotional approach in serious plays."

In 1946 Mr. Rattigan himself was in self-revealing mood in what was then probably the world's best theatrical periodical, *Theatre Arts*. Discussing "The Characters Make the Play," he stated—

"A play is born—for me, at any rate—in a character, in a background or setting, in a period or in a theme, never in a plot. I believe that in the process of a play's preliminary construction, during that long and difficult period of gestation before a line is put on paper, the plot is the last of the vital organs to take shape. . . .

"If the characters are correctly fashioned—by which I do not mean accurately representing living people but correctly conceived in their relationship to each other—the play will grow out of them. A number of firmly and definitely imagined characters will act—must act—in a firm and definite way. This gives you your plot. If it does not, your characters are wrongly conceived and you must start again. A plot, in fact, should come as a gift from the gods of drama, earned, it is true, by the laborious task of moulding character, background and theme but not (and I beg would-be playwrights—particularly retired civil servants—to listen to me), *not* casually picked up from the floor of memory as 'an idea for a play'."

And, then, after much more of interest: "But the reader may object . . . and say: 'All this may be true of *The Winslow Boy*, *Flare Path*, and *After the Dance*, your serious plays, perhaps even of *O Mistress Mine*, which was serious comedy. But what about your farces, *French Without Tears* and *While the Sun Shines*? In farce, plot is everything, character nothing. How do you explain that away?'" The playwright answers lucidly and follows cogent reasoning. His belief is in a formula for farce "which, though extremely simple, has not up to now been generally followed." Here is his *credo*—

"I believe in the farce of character . . . if the plot, however extreme, is at the very beginning rooted in character, if . . . the people are conceived before their story, it is possible with a little forcing to mould the plot into the most extravagant and farcical shape without exciting the audience's disbelief. And I think that an audience feels grateful towards a play that gains its continuous laughter without stretching its credulity. Even in farce it likes to be *made to believe* in what it sees happening on the stage; and what, after all, is the theatre but the game of make-believe?"

Yes, what, after all, and what differences in make-believe, for example, in Mr. Rattigan's demonstrated range from *French Without Tears* to his brilliant 1952 success at the Duchess Theatre with *The Deep Blue Sea*. There is certainly make-believe, but with plus or minus values. Make-believe for "pure" entertainment, whatever that may be, is different from make-believe for direct or indirect propaganda purposes. Again, the make-believe that is "manufactured" to influence in specific manner is different in type and texture from the make-believe that seeks to strike through emotion, or instinct, or inspiration, or imagination, or exaltation. The theatre, in short, presents a recurring problem just as, incessantly, it challenges the validity of the pessimists' cry of woe, "the theatre is dying" —a state of serious illness that has persisted with inconclusive results throughout the ages.

Importance of the Audience

The audience has its wishes, rights, obligations, and rewards. The critic in the theatre, like the theatrical speculator or the idealist in the theatre, is not always aware of what an audience demands. Many are the reasons why any particular play is accepted for production. These have a bearing on what the average theatregoer has the opportunity to see, and they are, in part, an explanation of wide disparities in the quality of the theatrical entertainment that managements provide.

The critic in the theatre probably knows more than theatre-goers about the stresses and strains that often precede the production and performance of a play and can express his approval or disapproval of the plays that he appraises professionally. An example of critics' power created interest in 1951 when there was a chorus of condemnatory criticism of the farcical comedy by Charles Lincoln, *Storks Don't Talk*, produced at the Comedy Theatre, London. It "ran" for three unusual nights. I was present on the second night. The gallery was closed and police were present. On the first night galleryites started booing three minutes after the rise of the curtain. Mischa Auer, who was the "star" of the production, stated subsequently in *Reynolds News*: "Actually, *Storks Don't Talk* is not the biggest flop I have appeared in. Not even the biggest flop ever. There was a musical comedy put on in New York in 1941 called *The Lady Comes Across*. It cost £50,000 to put on, and it had everything, including me. We opened on a Friday night. On Saturday afternoon we gave a free show to the theatre staff's kids. The show folded up in the evening."

In 1952 Bruce Walker's *Lion's Corner*, which was performed in the provinces for six weeks, was produced at St. Martin's

and withdrawn after one performance. There is no method
of gauging in advance and with scientific precision the response
of the theatregoing public. If there were, one-performance
runs or unprofitable short runs would be avoided.

Although the critic in the theatre may "kill" a specific
production now and again by strongly adverse criticism that
circulates in influential circles, he has little, if any, power to
alter the trend of the speculative selections of plays that are
made. Ultimately theatregoers are the human beings whose
individual and collective action is the decisive factor. But not
always. Occasionally theatregoers with specialized tastes
would like to see the performance of a play that cannot pass
the censor of stage plays; from time to time a worthwhile
production has a longer "life" than it would have if its continuance depended solely upon the revenue obtained through
the box-office: it is subsidized because those with the power
of patronage through financial support consider it to be of
artistic, dramatic, histrionic, educational, cultural, or other
significance.

In whatever perspective the theatre is placed, theorizing
about it is concerned with the multifarious activities which
start with the creative mind at work on the raw material of the
stage and end when the final curtain has descended upon that
raw material which, since its creation, has been moulded and
shaped by expert hands to make it attractive to theatregoers
as members of an audience. Who or what they are exactly
challenges conclusive definition by either the experts or the
business men of the theatre. Mr. Ashley Dukes once expressed
the opinion: "There is no shadow of reason in regarding them
(audiences) as anything but a gathering of individuals with
individual tastes." But the late John Drinkwater, not only a
poet in the theatre but a playwright who deepened interest in
biographical plays and who was partly responsible for the
fashionable trek of theatregoers from the West-End to the
Lyric at Hammersmith in 1919, to see his *Abraham Lincoln*,
wrote in one of his books:[1] "We playgoers then, are admittedly
separate individuals as we sit in the theatre; we do not wholly
lose our identity. The individual may hardly even be conscious

[1] *The Gentle Art of Theatre-going.*

that there is anyone else in the theatre besides himself and the players. He may be sincerely convinced that his impressions are not affected by his fellow playgoers, and that his judgment is being exercised in isolation. It is probable that under cross-examination almost every playgoer would admit this to be his view of his own experience. And yet there is definitely an energy at work in the theatre that cannot be accounted for by the fact that a large number of individuals have assembled not only with a common intention of seeing a particular play, but also with a common faculty for preserving their mental and emotional dependence. This energy is The Audience, and like Cowper's Jehovah, it moves in a mysterious way; mysterious, indeed, beyond the full understanding of any one of its component minds. My own theory, which I do not advance dogmatically, but after as close an investigation of the subject as I can manage, is that in a gathering of spectators in the theatre two separable activities are at work; the one governed by the emotions, the other by the reason; the one yielding and receptive, the other reserved and sceptical; the one discarding experience, the other testing by it. . . . My point is that there is, apart from individual spectators, such a thing as The Audience, that it is incorporated into a unit by the most elementary appeal of the theatre, and that its suffrage, often disregarding the opinions of individuals who themselves have nevertheless helped to bestow it, may establish a play to the tune of a million pounds' profit. . . . In the theatre money is made by a great variety of plays, but it is never made by a play that does not first of all establish contact with The Audience as an organism distinct from its individual members."

The more deeply theatregoers as such are thought of, the more obvious it becomes that they are important. The box-office test of the professional theatre is one piece of evidence. "Will it pay?" is a question that successive audiences answer, either consciously or unconsciously. Audiences have a definite contribution to make to the success of a theatrical performance and it is measurable in different ways. Once they are inside the theatre they may appear to be passive, understanding though unresponsive, superficially pleased but inwardly disappointed. Actors and actresses not only know of but also feel the presence of the audience. In certain types of entertainment they "play to the audience." This can be as undesirable as would be any attempt by the players to ignore the audience. The producer, in advance of a play's public performance, does his best to anticipate audience reaction, and some of his directions to the cast are, rightly or wrongly, influenced by his anticipations. Sometimes his theories are wrong. He thinks that a specific line, a carefully prepared important situation, a pointed rejoinder, are certain to create laughter-response in the audience, and on the first-night experiences surprise. The audience remains passive, but, unexpectedly, becomes expressive and applauds a different line, a situation that seemed to be relatively commonplace, an ordinary remark the entertainment value of which was unforeseeable during rehearsals.

There is no infallible method of ensuring in advance the correct or desired reaction to a player's performance or of anticipating correctly whether an audience will accept with enthusiasm or reject in disappointment any particular production or aspect of it. Dr. C. E. M. Joad had a story of the first night of *Fanny's First Play*, the success of which greatly widened Shaw's reputation, and one of Shaw's biographers, Hesketh Pearson, a similar story of the first night of *Arms and the Man*. Enthusiastic and prolonged applause and cries of "Author" followed the fall of the final curtain. Shaw eventually appeared and held up his hand for silence, during which one theatregoer, in the gallery, took advantage of the chance to make a particularly sibilant hiss as effective as possible. It made Shaw look up, smile, and remark: "My dear sir, I thoroughly agree with you. But who are we among so many?"

Robert Speaight is clear-cut on the audience as the ultimate arbiter:[1] "No play can come alive without actors to interpret, designers to decorate, and a producer to direct it. And the labours of all these people presuppose an audience. Without an audience they cannot be applauded and—what is perhaps more important—they cannot be paid. The audience is the final judge, and from its verdict there is no appeal. The audience makes or mars theatrical reputations and theatrical fortunes. When the determining appetite of audiences in this

[1] *Acting: Its Idea and Tradition.*

country is for the best that the Theatre can give them, the Theatre will cease to disappoint the nobility of its vocation. And not till then."

It may well be that the critic in the theatre holds opinions on the play that are sharply different from those of the majority of theatregoers who are present. If he does, when he writes he will make his own position clear, and also make it equally clear that many of the audience seemingly held different views from his on the quality and spirit of the play in performance, for if the critic is not sympathetic, his sincerity, a most valuable asset, can easily lead to aridity and distortion—from the point of view of the average theatregoer.

CHAPTER IX

THE CRITIC'S SINCERITY

THE critic in the theatre, invited to see the public performance of a play and to appraise it in print, becomes a
member of the audience, but not so readily and so completely
a member of the community of theatregoers as the majority
of the men and women who are present. Their attitude of
mind makes them more responsive than the critic to the traffic
of the stage. Their expectations are probably higher than his,
their knowledge is probably more superficial, their readiness
to be entertained more alert. Their theatregoing, with
relatively few exceptions, is spasmodically but hopefully
organized. The theatre is a place of entertainment, and they
pay to enter it, confident, perhaps, that they are bound to
spend an enjoyable evening as onlookers; disappointed,
mildly or keenly, if when they leave the play was not to their
liking, a "star" actress or actor not what they had been led to
expect from the publicity, or the players as a cast had had to
pretend to bring to life aspects of life that were too exaggerated,
or distorted, or devitalized to arouse genuine interest in them.

It is unlikely that these theatregoers will have read the
serious literature of drama and the stage. It is, indeed, likely
that their views of the contemporary theatre and of what goes
on inside it will be coloured by popular journalism. Every
theatre audience will include a percentage of theatregoers
whose self-selected interests impel them to read about the
theatre and stage: dramatists, producers, and players. Some
will discuss as members of student-groups, literary and debating
societies, etc., the place of the theatre in contemporary life,
the lives and the works of modern dramatists, the relationship
of drama to education, to religion, to literature, to politics, and
to other important and relevant subjects.

I do not wish to suggest that the average theatregoer is a
dunderhead who knows little or nothing about the theatre, in
order that the importance of the critic in the theatre may

plausibly be emphasized and exaggerated so that he appears
to be a very superior person. The wish is merely to place him
in a perspective that shows him to be different, principally
because his activities as a practising professional critic impel
him to acquire special knowledge, to understand the alphabet
of dramatic and theatrical production—all those aspects that
have been surveyed in previous chapters—to appraise what
is presented from the stage for the entertainment of the general
public, and to assess values about the bases of which there are
wide differences of opinion, even among his professional
colleagues.

What is of first-class importance is the critic's sincerity. It
is important when he has to express appraisement forthrightly
and courageously. To express it when it is pleasant to all
those who have contributed to theatrical entertainment—I
reiterate, playwright, producer, players, specialists behind the
scenes, and audience—and when it is founded on sincerity is
easy. When, in sincerity, it must be unfavourable and
unpleasant, even painful to sensitive people, the critic in the
theatre is faced with a temptation to compromise that he must
resist.

From his study, reading, and training for his work, and the
experience that he has gained in performing it, he has selected
and accepted a set of first principles of criticism that he applies
fearlessly and irrespective of consequences. This is not tanta-
mount to saying that what the critic, as a young man, thinks,
knows, feels, must remain static throughout life. The purpose
is to pinpoint sincerity as the keynote of sound criticism, while
recognizing that sincerity is not enough. Prejudices may
persist, personal taste may remain unchanged, additional
knowledge may fortify and consolidate convictions. Progress
towards maturity and wisdom is, however, likely to introduce
modifications and refinements, if not fundamental revolutionary
changes. Deliberately to harmonize one's opinions, sincerely
held, with equally sincere but conflicting opinions held by
others merely for the sake of producing harmony, is neither
intellectually honest nor desirable in the everyday practice of
criticism. Voltaire thought *Hamlet* "a rude and barbarous
piece—such a work as one might suppose to be the fruit of

the imagination of a drunken savage." Contemporary critics who are Shakespearean specialists would not endorse Voltaire's view. But analysis of the personal preferences and the continuously held convictions of these critics will reveal that there is much that is sound in Peter Ustinov's preface to a volume published in 1950. He wrote:[1] "The critics, the analysers, the professors are more intelligent than they have ever been, and that again is a drawback, especially as there are so many of them. Much is talked; much is written; much is attacked and defended; little is created; and contemporary civilization, with its love of Brains-Trusts, of magazine digests, of short cuts to knowledge, of quizzes, of lectures, has developed into a potent challenge to the creative artist, because it is confusing his simple and fundamental issues." This was the challenging statement of a playwright-player.

Mr. Ivor Brown, eminent critic, a specialist in the sensitive and appropriate use of language, in Shakespeare's plays and their performance, and in other cultural and literary aspects of life, commenting on this statement, wrote in *The Observer*: "I often feel, when I am invited to speak, write, debate, or play the Universal Answerer in a quiz, that we may not be so much helping the artist by this eternal theorizing as getting in his light. Of course, few artists dislike being turned into news, and the publicity must obviously help in one way. But all this supposed wisdom from above may tempt the public to have all its judgments handed out, to sit back, to go to the book-shop, the concert-hall, the art gallery or the theatre by proxy. Criticism, with its valuations, is there to stimulate patrons of the arts by lively and intelligent writing or speaking: it is not there to create instructed absentees. The public's proper line is to use criticism as judgments on which to sharpen its own judgment and that means having a look at the things which critics destructively analyse or comprehensively damn. Ustinov adds—

> Produce a work now, the battalions of highly intelligent theorists will settle on it, parasitically using its substance to spin their devious patterns in the air.

When I accept Ustinov's opinion that all this can be muddling

[1] *Plays About People.*

and baffling to authors I am not trying to put myself and colleagues out of work. But the public must not overlook the creator while it listens to the hubbub of the rival analysts."

It has been said that it makes all the difference in the world whether Truth is placed in the first place or in the second. The placing of Truth, or of what is accepted as Truth, is related to the art of criticism. Many people do not care to see themselves as they really are; they prefer to hear themselves spoken of as they think they are, or written about in similar vein. They like to have their prejudices respected and dislike vigorous and adverse critical handling, especially by critics who can see things in clear perspective, and give expression to their opinions—hence the widespread dislike of the critical attitude. It is not so much that people object to justice being done to their opponents; it is that for their very existence they must be given the benefit of any doubt. It is not enough for the critic to say that human beings are nine parts gold and one part dross, for the nearest part is that one part. The demonstration of the hollowness of belief, it was suggested by one writer, Ford Madox Hueffer, is what is dreaded most.

One definition of criticism is "the art of judging, especially in literature or the fine arts," a secondary definition being "a critical judgment or observation," and the critic is defined as one skilled in estimating the quality of literature or artistic work, with sundry other definitions, one of which is "a fault finder."

The idea that the critic must necessarily be a censorious person dies hard. When someone expressed an antagonistic opinion Johnson retorted: "Why, no, Sir; this is not just reasoning. You *may* abuse a tragedy, though you cannot write one. You may scold a carpenter who has made you a bad table, though you cannot make a table. It is not your trade to make tables." That, said John Drinkwater, is the critic's Declaration of Rights.

Intellectual Honesty in Criticism

If the critic in the theatre holds fast to intellectual honesty and gives direct and lucid expression to his opinions, he is certain to hurt the sensitive playwright, or the producer, or the players from time to time, unless they, equally honest, grant that he is a privileged member of the audience invited to be present in order to exercise his critical faculty to the best of his knowledge and ability. None the less, it is, perhaps, human nature for people who have done their best and failed to earn appreciation or even approval to be resentful rather than grateful. Relatively few acknowledge indebtedness in the generous spirit that marks the author's note in the printed version of *The Cocktail Party*: "I wish to acknowledge my indebtedness to two critics. To Mr. E. Martin Browne, who was responsible for the first production of this play at the Edinburgh Festival, 1949; for his criticism of the structure, from the first version to the last; for suggestions most of which have been accepted, and which, when accepted, have all been fully justified on the stage. And to Mr. John Hayward, for continuous criticism and correction of vocabulary, idiom, and manners. My debt to both of these censors could be understood only by comparison of the successive drafts of this play with the final text."

Expertness in the critic in the theatre does not inevitably make those who are adversely criticized readily accept his criticism as the hallmark of the expert in action. Their doubt of its validity, indeed, is much more likely to suggest that they would endorse, if called upon to do so, a special application of the words of Scripture: "Whom he would he slew, and whom he would he kept alive. Whom he would he raised up and whom he would he put down."

Shaw as a critic in the theatre long before he became a playwright with an international reputation—he contributed to *The Saturday Review* between the years 1895 and 1898—was a deliberate and ruthless destroyer of popular ideals, beliefs, superstitions, and prejudices. He was, in short, an iconoclastic critic who quickly got himself noticed and, in turn, severely criticized. Later, when making his apology for the appearance of his criticism in print, he warned his readers that what they were about to study was "not a series of judgments aiming at impartiality, but a siege laid to the theatre of the XIXth Century by an author who had to cut his own way into it at the point of the pen, and throw some of its defenders into the moat." Shaw in those days had opportunities that are denied the critic in the theatre today.

Modern journalism has revolutionized the methods of dealing with the criticism of plays. Readers of the popular Press, with notable exceptions, have to be satisfied, even when they are deeply interested in the theatre, with a concisely written news paragraph that contains little more than the title of the play, the name of the theatre in which it is performed, a brief indication of the story (sometimes not even this), and the names of the principal actors and actresses, with adjectival colouring to indicate praise or blame; even these details are not invariably given. In these circumstances, there is rigorously limited scope for the brilliance of a Shaw to have its reflection in the popular Press. "His criticisms still live," wrote James Huneker of Shaw's work, adding:[1] "They are as alive today as a decade ago, a sure test of their value; theatrical chronicling is seldom of an enduring character. It is the man ambushed behind the paragraph, the Shaw in the woodpile, with his stark individuality, that makes these criticisms delightful, and irritating and suggestive. . . . All criticism is personal, and neither academic nor impressionistic criticism should be taken too seriously. . . . The main point is—particularly in dramatic criticism—whether the writer holds our attention. Otherwise his work has no excuse for existence. Be as profound as you please—but be pleasing. Nature abhors an absolute; and there is no absolute in dramatic criticism."

Although the critic in the contemporary theatre has not the best possible chance to apply his special knowledge in print in newspapers and periodicals, many critics have made important contributions to the literature of drama, the theatre, and criticism. Moreover, through one channel of communication, the radio, expert opinions on aspects of drama and the theatre can be heard, and the increasing provision of facilities for education for leisure and pleasure has resulted in the sharpening of the critical faculty of many people, these tending, perhaps, to increase the number of superficial thinkers and to reduce "the number of those who undergo the fatigue of judging for themselves."

[1] *Dramatic Opinions and Essays.*

What, then, is the function of the critic in the theatre? In a sentence: to formulate personal opinions on the theatrical entertainment that is provided, and to give sincere expression to them.

This is not so simple as it may appear on first reading. My own interest in the theatre (as I have pointed out) began to canalize when, as a newspaper reporter, I volunteered to see a theatrical performance and to write about it because none of my colleagues was interested. Subsequently, whenever they could, they placed me under the obligation to write about plays and players. I was ill-equipped for my task and tried to remedy it by specialization. I was one of a number of journalists who, at that time, had to write about drama and the stage without knowing very much about them. Moreover, special knowledge, had it been possessed, could not have been used. Commercial and other considerations were stumbling blocks in the way of candid criticisms. Our opinions, individual and collective, were of little, if any value, in journalistic practice. But also at the time there were others who were making and moulding thought on drama and the theatre, critics whose writings on playwrights, plays, actors, actresses, productions, and performances were as important then—they still have importance—as the writing that was done by writers of the past such as A. B. Walkley, William Archer, and Bernard Shaw. Any scroll of outstanding dramatic critics of the twentieth century could include these (and other) names: James Agate, Percy Allen, E. A. Baughan, Beverley Baxter, G. W. Bishop, W. J. Bishop, Ivor Brown, J. M. Bulloch, Sydney W. Carroll, Harold Conway, A. V. Cookman, W. A. Darlington, Harris Deans, Paul Dehn, Alan Dent, M. Willson Disher, St. John Ervine, Richard Findlater, J. T. Grein, Hubert Griffith, Lionel Hale, Harold Hobson, Philip Hope-Wallace, Ralph E. Loveless, S. R. Littlewood, P. L. Mannock, Desmond McCarthy, C. E. Montague, Charles Morgan, Matthew Norgate, John Parker, Gale Pedrick, C. B. Purdom, F. A. Rice, Alan Pitt Robins, E. F. Spence, Clement Scott, John Shand, Ernest Short, Frances Stephens, J. C. Trewin, Kenneth Tynan, H. M. Walbrook, Bernard Weller, A. E. Wilson, and Geoffrey Whitworth.

The critic in the theatre, fulfilling his function by formulating genuine opinions to which he subsequently gives expression, must be an interpreter. "Criticism," said Carlyle, "stands like an interpreter between the inspired and the uninspired, between the prophet and those who hear the melody of his words, and catch some glimpse of their material meaning, but understand not their deeper import." "This," wrote the well known American critic, George Jean Nathan,[1] thought of by some as the G.B.S. of the States: "is the best definition that I know of. It defines without defining; it gives into the keeping of the interpreter the hundred languages of art and merely urges him, with whatever means may best and properly suit his ends, to translate them clearly to those that do not understand; it sets him free from the very shackles which Carlyle himself, removing from art, wound in turn about him."

Interpretation creates difficulties. There is a library of works that are designed to interpret Shakespeare and his plays. How many differing interpretations does the library contain? One outstanding critic in the theatre during the first quarter of the twentieth century, William Archer, was thought by some of his colleagues to be unscientifically biased in some of his attitudes towards the Elizabethans. Yet he was rational in mind and conscientious in service to the theatre. He even learned Norwegian in order to deal with, and to defend against the fulminations of his colleagues, and notably of Clement Scott, Henrik Ibsen, whose name, it is now clearly seen, the criticism of the time etched more deeply on the scroll of master dramatists.

Absolutism in Criticism

A warning against the dangers of absolutism in criticism is still registered by a re-reading of what some of the critics wrote about Ibsen and his plays. There are still critics who share Archer's views on the Elizabethans; critics who disagree about the qualities of Restoration drama compared with contemporary drama; critics who range themselves on the side of purity of form; critics who are biased in favour of ideas irrespective of the form in which they are contained. I

[1] *The Critic and the Drama.*

remember that A. B. Walkley, one of Archer's contemporaries, writing on the laws of change, stated:[1] "Our playbills have for some time shown a tendency to burst the old bonds of nomenclature. One dramatist labels his plays 'pleasant' and 'unpleasant'; another selects the novel epithet 'uncomfortable.' The truth is that the old descriptions of 'tragedy,' 'comedy,' and 'farce' have long since been found unsuitable; plays have run from one category into the other, or have proved, in the existing conditions of language, wholly nondescript. Criticism —always leaning to the conservative side—has girded at the dramatists, as though they were to blame. Even today critics will be found objecting that 'the author has called his play a comedy, whereas it is obviously a farce,' or that 'this so-called tragedy is nothing but a melodrama.' Such objections are really uncritical; or, at any rate, they are directed to the wrong address, ignoring as they do the patent fact that the growth of names never keeps pace with the growth of things."

Unlike Archer's attitude towards the study of Norwegian, Walkley's retort, when he was advised to master German so that he would be able to study Schiller in the original, was that not to learn German was to make easier his avoidance of Schiller in the original!

Not only nomenclature but also a play title can have a bearing on the style in which a criticism is written. As an example, this is how *The Times* critic in the theatre dealt with the production of Thomas Brown's *The Hat Trick* at the Duke of York's Theatre in May, 1950: "The comedy is perfunctory. Happily, there is nothing perfunctory in Miss Gladys Cooper's playing of the middle-aged lady who practises on husband, daughter, and daughter's presumptuous suitor the guile that made her in youth England's most deadly woman bowler.

"If not unaware of the weakness of the comedy, she is apparently quite indifferent to it; she has her part, she enjoys playing it, and she knows how to play it for rather more than it is worth. The drawing-room carpet is plainly the deadest of wickets, offering not the slightest encouragement to spin. No matter; she keeps throughout the evening an impeccable

[1] *Drama and Life.*

length and succeeds in imparting to the slowest of balls a suggestion of bite. Even when she picks up an actual cricket ball and arranges her fingers reminiscently about it, we are ready to believe that the arrangement is taken from an action photograph of Mailey's hand; in other words, it is a performance polished to the last detail." Then figurative language changes: "The rest of the company, with the exception of Mr. Richard Leech, seem to be adrift in a sea of unsolved problems." But there is a return to the nomenclature of cricket: "Somehow Mr. Leech makes good his part of the illusion; but Mr. . . . can get no farther than suggesting such a comfortable literary tradesman as Sir Max Beerbohm might draw. That he has any serious intention of doing anything more drastic than take a day off at Lord's never appears for a single moment; never was batsman less worthy of bowling so full of subtlety. . . . But ill-defended as are the wickets, it is a pleasure to watch England's deadliest woman bowler in action."

Shaw under the editorship of Frank Harris became dramatic critic of *The Saturday Review* in 1894 at £6 a week, twice the paper's usual remuneration, with the promise of a free hand, no contributions to be "cut" without consultation. From this position he developed "his strenuous leadership in drama criticism and eloquent championship of the cause of Ibsen." Shaw and Archer saw eye to eye with each other on Ibsen much more easily than they did on playwriting. When Archer, who wrote one of the best analytical books on playmaking, told Shaw that he could "construct a play but could not write dialogue," Shaw replied: "I can write dialogue by the thousand yards, but construction means nothing to me. So do you go ahead with your construction and I'll guarantee the dialogue." Archibald Henderson's comment is:[1] "Thus the collaboration began. It was an odd team: Archer, with an encyclopaedic knowledge of the world's drama, a naïve love for it, unbounded admiration for the 'well-made piece' in the Scribe-Dumas *fils* manner, and an inventive faculty of the feeblest; Shaw, with a genius for clever and witty sayings, which he had developed by years of platform speaking, and

[1] *Bernard Shaw: Playboy and Prophet.*

with the utmost scorn for plays with plots, which he lumped
with artificial flowers and clockwork mice. Collaboration
promised strange results." But it was short-lived! To recall
this incident from the past serves to bring out the inevitability
of the clash of opinions among experts. Is the position different
today?

It is not surprising that widely differing opinions on Shaw's
plays are still held. Most of his works were written deliberately
to provoke controversy. What of the reception given to the
plays of a playwright-poet, T. S. Eliot, whose outlook on life
is quite different from that which Shaw, the playwright-
propagandist, held? One of the "theatrical events" of 1950
was the production of *The Cocktail Party* at the New at the
beginning of May. This is a play by an author whose awareness of the desirability of introducing poetry into the theatre
without permitting it to oust prose has persisting influence.
Were the critics' opinions on this play unanimous? Of course
not! Here are quotations from the two Sunday newspapers
that allot space with a relatively generous hand.

It is a good recipe for success in the theatre to take one of the
oldest and never-failing darlings of the public, Cinderella or the
Mysterious Stranger, and then attach him or her to a current
vogue of thought about which discussion is general. In *The
Cocktail Party* Mr. T. S. Eliot has given us the Stranger and
attached him to psychiatry. The ever-passing Third-Floor Back
has now become a First-Floor Freud or, more exactly, a mental
medico who goes to the best tailors, "crashes" the best parties,
likes gin and water, and can wear a film-star's smile. So here,
indeed, is something for everybody. There is sex-trouble and
cocktail-chatter for those who like lounge-hall comedy: there is
verse—or so it seems when you see it printed—for those who like
the New Noise in the theatre, but the verse is so unrecognizable
as such that the Prose Party need not be alarmed. Ninety per
cent of the audience, unless previously instructed, will take the
text as normal except in one passage. The element of mystery
has been lessened since Edinbu.gh. The enigmatic "Guardians"
have less prominence now. The inexplicable Libation remains,
a delight to those who dote on confusion in the arts, so that they
may go away and discuss the meaning afterwards. To say
"inexplicable" is no discourtesy, for has not Mr. Eliot explained
that works of art have only the meaning which the public confers
on them, a creed of cloudiness much observed by the minor

poets today? . . . Was there ever such a shrewd assortment of
Fair Shares in Drama, something for all parties and so an ample
theme for supper-time debate? . . . As now performed, the
play seems to be clearer and more human than in the Edinburgh
production of last year.[1]

. . . Celia . . . is a saint: and for the saints the petty fulfil-
ments of commonplace existence are not enough. She must
tread the precipice edge, and put her hand in the fire.

One would expect Mr. Eliot, whose fineness of mind and depth
of religious conviction are not in doubt, here to be at his best. He
is not. He is strongest in the most trivial parts of his play. . . .

Is *The Cocktail Party* a great play? It is at least near enough to
greatness to make the question worth asking. It comes from a
mind acute as Sir Isaac Newton's that wishes to write like
Dostoevsky, and succeeds at its best but not its most ambitious
in doing as well as Jane Austen.[2]

Here, too, is a quotation from one of the popular London
morning papers that gives its critic in the theatre scope to
express himself in print—

Let my reader understand me, please. It gives me no kind of
perverse glee to be a thorn in Mr. Eliot's side, or to be a fly in
the ointment of praise which has been handed to him, in a pot,
on the occasion of this play's production in London now, as in
Edinburgh last August.

Far from feeling gleeful, I am full of what—a few years ago—
we were in the habit of calling alarm and despondency.

The critic in me is alarmed that a play so deplorably weak in
playcraft should be hailed as something like a masterpiece.

The critic in me is despondent when wilful obscurity is greeted
as subtlety, when affected persiflage passes for wit, when plain
flat prose cut into lines of arbitrary length is loosely given the
name of poetry. . . .

Mr. Eliot insists, in both programme and printed version, that
his play is a "comedy." As comedy, then, let it first of all be
judged.

In contrivance this comedy has rather less ingenuity than a
stage-struck schoolgirl might show in a first attempt at playwriting.

The telephone is seldom silent. People come and go and return
—either into a waiting taxi or into the kitchen—for the unlikeliest
and the stupidest reasons. The clumsiness of these artifices kept
me gasping repeatedly.

[1] Ivor Brown in *The Observer*.
[2] Harold Hobson in *The Sunday Times*.

The so-called and much-praised wit consists largely of the sort of verbal repetition which can only be heard in the conversation of the more bloodless sort of intellectuals when they are anxious to unbend.

In the first act alone I counted no fewer than fifteen examples of this device. Here is a perfectly typical, fair and characteristic instance:

Julia: *The only man I ever met who could hear the cry of bats.*
Peter: *Hear the cry of bats?*
Julia: *He could hear the cry of Bats.*
Celia: *But how do you know he could hear the cry of bats?*
Julia: *Because he said so. And I believed him.*

If that is witty dialogue, I am beginning to hear bats in my own belfry.

The play attains some genuine subtlety only in the first scene of the second act.

Here, too, the writing takes on a quality and a dignity which is almost completely lacking everywhere else. Here alone do I understand the Eliotolaters accepting their fine poet as a fine dramatist as well. . . .

Molière's Jourdain discovered that we all speak prose; and in course of time Mr. Eliot has discovered that we all speak verse. But what very prosaic and prosy verse it can be, to be sure! [1]

Did the book critics adopt different attitudes, have conflicting opinions on the play? Basically, no. An actor (Robert Speaight) reviewed three plays by J. P. Sartre and *The Cocktail Party* for *Drama*, the quarterly theatre review published by the British Drama League. He made these points—

If one may suggest, broadly speaking, that *Murder in the Cathedral* was a liturgical drama, and *The Family Reunion* a classical drama, each discovering its essential pattern in traditional models, then *The Cocktail Party* may be described as a modern comedy. The setting and psychology are familiar to a contemporary playgoer; the solution is far less familiar and far less acceptable. . . . What places *The Cocktail Party* in a category apart is that between the clinking of glasses and banter of conversation we overhear, sometimes in disguised accents and sometimes with theological clarity, the overtones of traditional wisdom. . . . *The Cocktail Party* has with some reason been described as an Existentialist play. Eliot sees what Sartre sees— but he sees further. . . . there remains enough in common between Eliot and Sartre for *The Cocktail Party* to be profoundly

---

[1] Alan Dent in *News Chronicle.*

misunderstood, and therefore appreciated for the wrong reasons.
Incomprehension is already busily at work.

We must admit that Eliot has not made the going easy.
Wishing to address himself to contemporary man in terms that
contemporary man will understand, he has hidden the operation
of grace under a play of secular symbols. . . . All Art is play,
and symbols are the poet's playthings. Eliot uses them here to
brilliant purpose, but will they, in fact, perform the office of
communication? . . .

For *The Cocktail Party*, though it is easier to listen to than *The
Family Reunion*, and more dramatically realized, is not any easier
to understand. Its Shaftesbury Avenue surfaces conceal their
secrets, and there will always be members of every audience who
will imagine they have come to see one play and find that they
have come to see another. There is, in fact, an element of
conjuring in Eliot's manipulation of his material, and this, like
other forms of practical joking, is always liable to give offence.

A poet, Louis Macneice, reviewing the book for *The Observer*,
wrote—

Poets in our time who wish to be playwrights only too often
make their primary aim the writing of plays *in verse*. This is very
much putting the cart before the horse. Verse dialogue has
certain great advantages over prose dialogue, but the dialogue
itself is more than its raiment or to put it differently, the verse
must be dramatic first and verse second. It is a great pity that
poets should be blind to this, since potentially they are better
equipped for dramatic writing than the ordinary prose-writer. . .

This play (*The Cocktail Party*) has proved that neither an extra
dose of "realism" nor an extra dose of comedy need mean short
rations. Where *The Cocktail Party* fails, failure is due not
to its chosen limitations but to certain deficiencies or certain
wrong emphases which could have been adjusted within those
limitations.

Finally, for illustrative purposes, T. C. Worsley, a critic of
one of the important weekly periodicals, *The New Statesman
and Nation*, opened on an interesting note—

A play is not fully "out"—Bernard Shaw and Henry James
agreed on this point—until we have both seen the stage production and had the text in our hands. By this test Mr. Fry's play
(*Venus Observed*) is now fully, Mr. Eliot's only half, produced—
except for those who saw it in Edinburgh and Brighton, or for the
Americans. (A state of affairs that was, of course, quickly
altered.) Yet if it is rather shaming to our theatre that New
York should applaud the newest play of our leading poet before

London can, the disgrace is more than offset by the ready welcome
which it has given to Mr. Christopher Fry. It was not many
years ago that verse plays were considered the least marketable
of all conceivable theatrical products. Now, not only do our
leading actors commission Mr. Fry to write for them, but the
public, too, flock to hear him. This reveals a spirit of adventur-
ousness all round—a willingness to take risks—that is something
new and hopeful in our theatre.

Mr. Eliot's play has had no less a success than Mr. Fry's where
it has been played. But then with *The Cocktail Party* he has taken
the greatest pains to build on an established model so as to catch
a wider audience. And indeed the first thing to be said about *The
Cocktail Party* is that with it he has succeeded in this aim. It is
difficult to judge how the text will strike those who have not seen
the production. But I who have can vouch for its being highly
effective with the kind of audience which probably does not read
(and would not necessarily enjoy if it did read) Mr. Eliot's
poetry. Only those who have not had to sit through in one year
as many badly built plays as a dramatic critic has to endure in
the average month would underestimate this quality. But this
success is achieved at a price. The text makes it clear that we
lose in depth and richness what we gain in ease and speed.

For postscript I quote again Alan Dent with a query—

Why must these poet-dramatists—Christopher Fry always
excepted—be so utterly without humour, and therefore be
without that sensibility that goes with that sense?

One asset of the critic in the theatre is his knowledge of what
drama has been, is, and perhaps may be. He knows how "to
place" dramatists, past and present. He knows that Aristophanes was the most important of Attic comedy writers and
that some suggest that he remains the world's greatest writer
in this vein; the critic knows that Aristotle's unities demanded
unity of place, of time (twenty-four hours), and of action; that
Sophocles, an Athenian tragic poet, and Aeschylus, known as
the father of Greek tragedy, were competitors and that the
judges preferred the junior Sophocles; that the "apron stage"
of the Elizabethan Age—the part of it between the stage
proper and the audience—has its counterpart in some modern
productions; that Shakespeare wrote in blank verse, that most
contemporary dramatists write in prose that is "stage speech,"
and that a few turn to poetry in reaction to naturalistic
dialogue; that Restoration drama was a drama of revolt in

search of a greater freedom relative to the Elizabethan drama;
that Robertson, Pinero, and Jones instituted another revolt,
against French influence, and in doing so laid the foundations
of the naturalistic drama of their successors, who themselves
were influenced by other foreign influences, and notably by
Ibsen, Strindberg, Hauptmann, Lessing, and Göethe.

These things, and many more, the critic in the theatre knows.
He knows, too, of the significance of the names of men whose
work made history in direction and production—Reinhardt,
and Gordon Craig, and William Poel, and Granville Barker.
He knows that style in acting today is different from what it was
at the turn of the century, and that, going farther back, the spirit
of the times as well as physical environment and conditions
were reflected in the styles that were then the vogue. He knows
what was written in the past by his predecessors in criticism,
by Pepys, Fielding, Leigh Hunt, Hazlitt, and Charles Lamb,
and by the critics in the theatre who either turned the direction
of the flow of modern drama or contributed towards its
evolution.

He knows that the audiences that saw Shakespeare's plays
at the Globe Theatre were different from, and paradoxically,
similar to the audiences—1,154 of them—which saw Terence
Rattigan's *While the Sun Shines*, which was produced at the
Globe Theatre on Christmas Eve, 1943. Historical details he
has in plenty. Therefore, he is the possessor of useful background information and foundational knowledge. Upon these
he draws for his appraisement of the dramatic and theatrical
entertainment to which he goes professionally, but, although
he knows much more than the average theatregoer about the
evolution of drama, the history of the theatre, of the presentation of plays and of the art of acting through the ages, of
audiences and their changing tastes with the March of Time,
he is also conscious of the necessity to revalue values every
time he enters a theatre.

The Critic's Role

The critic's role is that of an interpreter. His seeming
passivity clothes his sentient self. He accepts, momentarily,
Dr. Stockman's dictum that the strongest man is he who stands

alone, as he sits, one member of an audience of hundreds, and realizes that he is no more capable of being completely alone in the theatre than is any other member who sits round and about him. He formulates opinions built on foundations of special knowledge and its application, experiences individual taste, and yet admits into his assessment factors that are common to the audience as audience. He is a man or a woman with reasoned opinions on each of the units that comprise the whole, seeing in them primary, secondary, auxiliary, and illustrative material that must be woven into the pattern of reaction and evaluation that constitute his criticism or appraisement. He may be strongly individualized and allow strong prejudices to colour his judgment. He may be arrogant and permit his arrogance to do injustice to others. He may be sympathetic and kindly in character and disposition and lower sound standards in order to reduce the risk of hurting earnest and sensitive people. He may be an iconoclastic critic with an axe to grind in order to make his personal contribution to the advancement of a cause in which he believes. He may be an idealist, a dreamer, an evolutionist, who, knowing what is, represses or refines his expression of it in order to turn counsellor and advocate for what he thinks and believes ought to be in playwriting, production, acting, or audience. He may easily fit into any one of these categories or be the personification of a blend of several of them, or his own highly individualized attitude towards drama and the theatre may enable him to create for himself a unique category, distinctive and differentiated on a reasoned basis from that of any of his colleagues.

One certainty is that, whatever his type or category, he will not be accepted as an infallible critic by all who are interested in the appraised performance. He and his criticism will be discussed by those who are interested in drama and the theatre in very much the same way as discussion is made to proceed by Elmer Rice:[1] "In theatrical circles dramatic criticism was a subject of persistent and virulent controversy. In the past months Eric had read in the drama sections of the New York newspapers numerous articles and letters dealing with the function of the critic in the theatre. Authors and

[1] *The Show Must Go On.*

managers who had suffered at the hands of the critics denounced them in harsh terms; the critics, according to their natures, replied petulantly, facetiously, or apologetically; and play-goers frequently joined in, siding sometimes with the critics and sometimes with their attackers.

"The argument had no focus, for there were as many points of view as there were controversies. Some contended that the critic should confine himself to reporting the reactions of the first-night audience; some that he should record his own impressions, regardless of the audience's response. Others thought that criticism should be designed to guide the theatre-goer in his choice of plays; still others, that it was the duty of the critic to uphold the dignity of the drama and to judge plays by high standards of excellence. Eric inclined to the latter view, remembering that Anatole France had defined criticism as the adventures of a soul among masterpieces. His own tastes and criteria had been developed by reading the dramatic essays of Lamb, Hazlitt, and Coleridge, and of such late nineteenth- and early twentieth-century critics as Bernard Shaw, Max Beerbohm, Francisque Sarcey, C. E. Montague, Henry James, William Winter, Georg Brandes, William Archer, and James Huneker, as well as some more recent writers. But he had seen enough of the New York theatre to understand the difficulty of measuring it by the yardstick of perfectionism.

"One point on which there was general agreement was the direct and immediate relationship between the newspaper reviews and the popularity of the play; while instances could be cited of plays that had failed in spite of favourable reviews and of others that had become great successes in the face of critical condemnation, there could be no doubt that, in the main, good reviews meant a long run and bad ones an early closing. But there was great difference of opinion as to whether this was because the critics represented a fair cross-section of popular taste or because newspaper readers tended to regard a published review as a weighty and authoritative pronounce-ment rather than as the expression of one man's point of view. Why, it was frequently asked, should a huge investment of money, time and creative effort be jeopardized by the hastily formed judgment of an individual, who might lack the training or perception to make a valid appraisal or whose opinion might be coloured by prejudice, spite, or the fact that his dinner or his wife had disagreed with him? A curtailment of the power of critics was loudly demanded—though how this was to be accomplished was never very clearly stated. In fact, many of those who complained most bitterly about the undue influence of the press were responsible for further increasing the prestige of the critics by widely publicizing favourable reviews of which they happened to be the beneficiaries."

The hum of conversation in the foyer and in the auditorium during the intervals of a public performance, it is recalled, often includes the spontaneous "criticism" of the average theatre-goer. Should the critic in the theatre, when he overhears it, be influenced by it? When the average theatregoer reads in his or her newspaper a criticism or a notice of the play that has just been seen and, perhaps, thoroughly enjoyed, should he, or she, seek to adjust what was his or her genuine opinion to make it conform to that expressed by the critic in the theatre, the acknowledged expert, when he has written unfavourably about it? "How difficult it is," wrote E. F. S.,[1] "to tell even the relative truth; the absolute is out of the question. Suppose that the critic has come to the conclusion that he knows the truth about a play, with what is he to tell it? With language, of course—an appallingly bad piece of machinery, which grows worse and worse every day. When a number of critics have formed the same opinion about a piece, and all wish to say that it is good—a very bad term to employ—one will call it good, another very good; a third, exceedingly good; a fourth great; a fifth, splendid; a sixth superb; and so on till some reckless language-monger uses the state-occasion term—a 'work of genius.' How is the reader to guess that they all mean the same thing? Moreover, if they were to use identical words every reader would put a somewhat different meaning upon them.

" 'One of my greatest difficulties,' a famous physician once said,' lies in the fact that to a great extent I have to rely upon a patient's description of the nature and quantity of pain he or she has suffered from. One will speak of pain where another

----

[1] *Our Stage and Its Critics.*

employs the word agony; the third complains of intense torture; a fourth describes it as intolerable anguish; and a fifth says it hurts a little. Yet they all refer to the same thing. No wonder we are often at sea.'"

The critic in the theatre is not permanently "at sea!" Temporarily, though, he may have navigational doubts! These, however, are resolved when his analysis of the pros and cons of a public performance, made by the application of his specialized knowledge and experience, is undertaken and completed.

CHAPTER X

THE CRITIC'S CONTRIBUTION

ALTHOUGH there is plenty of evidence that drama marches with the times, and even gets ahead of them, and that methods of production, styles of acting, and the appeals of public performances change with the changing world, there is much less convincing evidence that the theatre, the home of drama, the workshop of actors and actresses, the playhouse of the people, succeeds in keeping pace with contemporary needs, or that some people with power, who might influence the development and progress and also control the direction the theatre should take in order to keep abreast of requirements, think of it as a highly desirable, if not essential, institution of modern society.

In an age of planning, which, in some degree, affects most human activities, the theatre itself survives as a symbol of an age that was, rather than as the symbol of a more glorious age that is in the making. Where it has not given way to more modern forms of public entertainment that are organized and housed for the amusement of the people, the theatre functions, almost without aid, against increasing handicaps, and caters for minority tastes and requirements.

It is true that in London, notwithstanding the changes in people's habits and hobbies that modern science has made possible, the theatre continues to attract large numbers of theatregoers, many from provincial regions from which the theatre as the contemporary home of professional plays has disappeared where once it flourished. But, relatively, the enthusiasm that it engenders, and the strength of the support that it receives, are not favourably comparable with those that promoters of other forms of public entertainment enjoy and from which they profit because they have to meet more spontaneous and more irresistible demands for facilities for pleasure-making. Visitors to London, especially those who live in places where they cannot conveniently attend dramatic and theatrical performances regularly, or even at all, and tourists from across the Atlantic (incidentally, in New York what happens on Broadway is sometimes reminiscent of what has happened in Shaftesbury Avenue) still think of London theatregoing as a desirable expression of social life. It is, however, undertaken for all sorts of reasons that have little, if anything, to do with aesthetic delights, which are not the only delights that spring from participation in theatregoing.

The average theatregoer who consults the advertisements in the national newspapers published in London is almost always likely to be in a position to see a dramatic or theatrical entertainment that is of significant merit. Chance, however, can easily lead to innocent and blind rather than deliberate and wilful support of play presentations which may be box-office "draws" for months and pay commercial enterprise that made them possible generous returns on invested capital, but which may also be performances that have slender claims to be included in the category of dramatic or theatrical art.

Theatregoers who decide "to see a show" because they have heard that it is "very good," or, perhaps, because an actor or actress in it is "making a hit," are not necessarily the victims of distorted publicity and false praise. They may be in the mood thoroughly to enjoy any dramatic or theatrical entertainment for which they are willing to pay, and, in the circumstances, their London theatregoing may legitimately be numbered among the best, if not the cheapest, of their holiday pleasures or of diversified evenings spent in search of amusement shared with numbers of unknown people. There is nothing inherently wrong in paying for something from which genuine pleasure is derived or which amuses. "The knocka-bout comedian may be more profitable than Hamlet. One good comedian is worth twenty bad Hamlets—if there is such a thing as a bad Hamlet. A good melodrama is better than a poor tragedy, a good comedy is second to no play of any description. Tragedy at its highest is man's picture of himself unconquerable in spirit, though his material affairs fall into utmost disaster. But comedy at its highest might be the view of the gods. . . . Tragedy is subjective, comedy is objective. Both are of extreme value: wisdom, I think, would not put one above the other; for to gain a view of the world approaching completeness they should be combined in the mind of the spectator. Here," avers Haleolt Glover,[1] "lies the latest dignity of melodrama, for in a rough-and-ready fashion melodrama does combine the human and the godlike view."

Like most people who are conveniently placed in a special category, theatregoers have opinions on what they want, and in their self-organization to get it they can be ingenious. So, too, can those who provide dramatic and theatrical entertainment. They are well aware that theatregoers have their likes and dislikes; that they do not like having their prejudices violently disturbed, or their convictions strongly challenged; that the majority of them enter the theatre for an evening's amusement and that many views of what amuses are held in all sincerity and with tenacity. In London, and outer London, with a population of millions, there are other types of theatregoers: those who are interested in experimentation and who support the work of organizations that are founded and that function for the advancement of dramatic and theatrical art. These organizations are, in some cases, short-lived. Their ideal is an incentive. They fail in the practical world, where pounds, shillings, and pence count for much, to attract support in sufficient strength to make continuance of their work possible. Some who are single-minded may suggest that this type of work makes little impression on the world of the theatre; that it is carried out by cranks, fanatics, theorists, who at best cater for coteries and cliques, and that the more they succeed the more is the theatre likely to be divorced from life. Also catering for coteries and cliques are the propagandists who think of their work as missionary work. They have a gospel to preach, a message to deliver, a dogma to popularize. They regard the theatre not so much as a playhouse where people are amused as a public building in which there is a stage that serves as a platform. Their conception of the place of the theatre in modern society is very different from that of those for whom some of the quintessence of enjoyable social life is to go to a West-End theatre to see a light comedy or a "musical."

[1] *Drama and Mankind.*

What the playwrights think drama should be must have a bearing on what the theatre must be in society. The popular view, which is likely to prevail, is that the playwright should write plays which, in performance, will entertain. A different view, which is also likely to persist among a very much smaller number of people, is that mere entertainment cannot hold exclusively a place of such predominant importance, and that the best entertainment has educational and cultural values intermixed. Difficulties of definition again confront any who would understand and define either attitude towards drama and the theatre.

Education is not the assimilation of facts and information. It is possible for an adult to have a sound grasp of the essentials of the business or profession in which he is engaged, and, at the same time, to be uneducated, or educated only in a very narrow sense. Vocational training leads to the acquisition of knowledge that is essential for the pursuit of a vocation, but pursuit does not necessarily enable the pursuer to live a full life. Education should teach people how to live. There are many aspects of life that must be touched and experienced before life can be said to be lived fully.

Aristotle defined drama in simple and concise terms. Drama, he contended, is imitated human action. It is helpful to bear in mind the broad fact that drama reveals and reflects humanity in its varied and varying associations and conditions. Art, it is well said, is a material creation of man which faithfully reflects the spirit of the age and its experiences, "the very body of the time, its form and pressure," as Shakespeare had it. Thought changes and develops, is revolutionized, and its changes, developments, and revolutions sooner or later constitute the material of which drama is made.

The connexion between drama and education becomes apparent. Education is a training in the art of living, and drama is the art that catches up the spirit of living, crystallizes thoughts and actions, illustrates, emphasizes, and illumines experiences. Elaboration of this line of thought brings out possible associations of drama and education and leads to the introduction of the problem of culture in a civilized community.

Civilization and Culture

"We see that culture is not simply music, literature, science, architecture, and so forth, but civilization itself," states R. C. Churchill:[1] "a form of life different from, and superior to, both the society of primitive peoples and the society of material progress. Man does not live by bread alone; and, so long as we do not use that argument as a pretext for cutting the bread ration of other people—'Bread for myself is a material question,' observes Berdyaev, 'bread for my neighbour is a spiritual question'—it is difficult to deny its truth. Man does not live, either, by the latest scientific appliances alone; a civilization cannot be called a culture if it is mainly preoccupied with the manufacture and use of these articles, though there is nothing to be said against them in themselves. 'For the enjoyment of art,' said Richard Jefferies, however (and his words are applicable to culture in general), 'it is first of all necessary to have a full belly.' Only after the belly has been filled, and other material wants supplied, is man ready to use his mind, to create or pursue such enjoyments as offer themselves to his spirit."

This quotation from a book on the subject of culture in Western Civilization—Mr. Churchill's sub-title is "A Polemic on Culture in the English Democracy"—reveals the complexity of modern society. What results can be expected from efforts that are exerted to raise the standard of life of people while not depressing the higher standards of those whose cultural background and status were unquestioned until the Industrial Revolution? What will be the sequel to the new concepts of social commentators whose theorizing causes new attitudes towards the organization of society to be adopted, and proclaims new aims as goals for civilization to reach? Consideration of these quotations often begins human conflicts.

"The first recorded use of the word 'culture' in its modern sense is 1510, just when capitalism began to get going. It was the time of the Revival of Learning and the Renaissance, and those two movements signify the very essence of culture for all educated people, even unto the present day. But it was not until the beginning of the nineteenth century, the period of the

---

[1] *Disagreements.*

Industrial Revolution, that culture became finally divorced from work. So long as people made things by hand, certain traditional ways of making them persisted, and were good. It was only when things began to be made by machines that the traditions inherent, as it were, in the minds and muscles of the handworker, finally disappeared. Unless the present economic system is abolished, its roots eradicated and all its intricate branches lopped, the first conditions for a democratic alternative to the fake culture of our present civilization are not satisfied. For this reason one cannot be very specific about the features of a democratic culture. Engineers and designers can make the working drawings for a motor-car, and granted the right kind of machinery they can be sure that the type of car they have designed will run when it is completed. But they cannot predict where the car will travel. A democratic culture," affirms Sir Herbert Read,[1] "is the journey a democratic society will make when once it has been established."

This digression is made deliberately. Whenever drama and the theatre are discussed seriously it is probable that before discussion has produced final decisions many tendentious statements will have been made. Some will think that dramatists should write to influence society directly; some that drama should be directly educational; some that theatrical entertainment should be provided for amusement only; some that it is possible to blend entertainment-education-culture without depreciating the basic values of any of the three. The primary concern here is with the theatre as an institution in modern society.

What is the modern theatre? What has the average theatregoer a right to expect of it? Some questions are worth reasking. Is the theatre an instrument of education? The home of culture? The place in which pleasure for the people is provided? A platform for propaganda? A pulpit for preachers? A cockpit where commercialists do battle for profit? An attractive haven to which the escapist retreats? A sounding-board for the poet? An Aladdin's cave in which colour and costume, dance and decoration, the feminine form and rhythmic, sensual, or melodious music make fanciful

[1] "To Hell With Culture" in *The Politics of the Unpolitical*.

appeal to the eyes and the ears of the easily entertained? An ivory tower that is entered by those who have resigned themselves to the persistence of what they regard as contentious contemporary problems that they wish to leave to others to solve?

These rhetorical questions raise issues that recur in circles where it is admitted that the theatre is a necessary social institution, and where, too, there are wide divergences of opinion on what exactly the institution itself should be, and what should be its legitimate and desirable functions in modern society.

Representative opinions expressed in the literature of the theatre are enlightening. What the experts and the specialists assert the theatre is, or should be, explains in part the conflicts of opinions on plays, play productions, and performances, conflicts which sometimes create confusion in the minds of ordinary theatregoers and raise doubts about the validity of criticism.

Should the material that ordinarily passes through the theatre be changed? Here is Roger Dataller's inquiring mind in action:[1] "The more one studies the Theatre, the more it becomes a source of increasing wonder that the eminently varied English industrial scene should for some prevailing reason have been completely boycotted. We are treated to plays dealing with murderers, anarchists, stockbrokers, Empire builders, dope addicts, statesmen, bookmakers, touts, and journalists—the fringe, so to speak, of the industrial field. The mines, the steel works, the mills, the foundries, the fisheries, are ignored. Why? Does it all boil down to the dress-suit complex?"

Wars and their aftermaths, revolutions and dictatorships, have had their reflections in the theatre. The desire for a change of accent in the directions indicated may not be as strong now as it was, say, shortly after the first political and economic revolutions in Russia.

Are the experts and the specialists who focus attention on the theatre and who seek to mould it to their ways helpful or harmful? Geoffrey Whitworth, who told the story, in *The*

[1] *Drama and Life.*

Making of a National Theatre, of the century-old campaign in
favour of a National Theatre, the foundation-stone of which
was laid on 13th February, 1951, sensed danger in expert and
specialist participation:[1] "Note that, whereas every other mode
of artistic apprehension is derived from an impulse that is less
than the whole sum of our impulses, the art of the stage relies
on the action of the complete human being, seen in the round,
and presented in its every facet and relation as the object of
our regard, and as the subject of our emotional response. No
wonder that men too strictly trained in one direction—men
like Charles Darwin, for instance—have been driven to confess
that the art of the stage means nothing to them, that they feel
a sense of actual discomfort when viewing a stage play. Such
is the curse that attends a too insistent specialization on the
intellectual side—a surfeit of the fruit of the Tree of Knowledge. So woe betide the specialist who, when he enters a
theatre, cannot forget that he is a specialist. Let him be a
plain man if only for an hour; else his lost soul will drive at
him from the outer darkness, and, sitting there in the stalls,
he will become as one made with boredom and disgruntlement."

Shaw's ideal theatre would be: "A factory of thought, a
prompter of conscience, an elucidator of social conscience, an
armoury against despair and dullness, and a Temple of the
Ascent of Man." Thinking on these lines, he was not alone.
". . . . when we see what an instrument of human enlighten-
ment the theatre can and should be, we cannot help lamenting
the degradation and timidity which have almost overcome it
today. Instead of being a soporific, it should be our perpetual
refreshment, goad, and gadfly, the vehicle for ideas of every
sort, however subversive, open alike to pure art, politics, and
propaganda, to experiment of every sort, with the utmost
freedom of theme and presentation. We should be able to
hear in it not only what we like but what we dislike. We
should be prepared for attacks on all our convictions, social
and moral. "If we are afraid to have our ideas challenged,"
contends L. A. G. Strong,[2] "it can mean only that our hold on
them is insecure, that we are afraid of losing them. We should

---

[1] *The Theatre of My Heart.*
[2] *Common Sense About Drama.*

never shrink from hearing blasphemy. Blasphemy, whether religious, scientific, or political, is a tonic shock, forcing us to test the reality of our beliefs."

This reminds me of the conclusion reached by Norman Marshall, who thought it worth while to attempt to make a record of the pioneer theatres in England during this century[1]—

"In the old days dwindling audiences were generally the reason for periodic outbreaks of speculation about 'What's wrong with the theatre.' Today, when audiences are larger and more enterprising than they have ever been before, there are not the buildings in which to accommodate them. There is little hope of any alteration in this state of affairs in the immediate future, and by the time it is possible to build more theatres most of the new audience built up during the war by C.E.M.A. and E.N.S.A. will have drifted away from the theatre again because of the lack of sufficient opportunities for play-going. It is unlikely that apart from the National Theatre any new theatres will be built in London during this century. . . . As property in the centre of London becomes more and more valuable it is likely that unless the Government takes action to prevent it many existing theatres will be sold at huge prices to be pulled down and rebuilt as hotels or business premises. As London theatres grow fewer rents will soar and prices of seats will have to be substantially increased to pay these rents. Theatregoing in the West-End will become so expensive that except for the very rich it will be confined mainly to 'a night out' for the celebration of some special occasion. . . . During the years which must elapse before municipal theatres can be built in the provinces a great responsibility rests on the repertory theatres. . . . If there are to be no more than a dozen theatres in London and only three or four repertories in the provinces capable of giving adequate productions of new plays, there is a real danger that the race of English dramatists may soon become almost extinct."

Plays, it is obvious, pass through the theatre whatever its state or condition during any given epoch or era, with the exception of those plays that none of the specialists who are

[1] *The Other Theatre.*

concerned with the provision of dramatic and theatrical entertainment thinks are suitable for profitable presentation.

The Living Theatre

The producers and the players react to the playwrights on the one hand, and, on the other, to the audiences. What is the contribution of the critic to progress in the theatre? Must the theatre progress? Must it reflect life? Portray life? Interpret life? Must thought be primarily of the creative genius who expresses himself as a playwright? Of the producer whose imaginative handling of the playwright's material reveals its qualities, good or bad, and emphasizes either or both? Of the players without whose aid the playwright's product would, in great measure, be stillborn? Of the audience with its varying reactions and evaluations of the traffic of the stage?

The critic in the theatre answers these, or similar, questions in accordance with his own attitude towards the theatre.

The playwright may disagree with the printed evaluation of his play. As a creative writer he himself may not be clear about what he has communicated by his writing. One of the criticisms of some of the work of T. S. Eliot is that it is obscure. Once when Shaw was asked to explain a passage in one of his plays he retorted that he himself didn't know its meaning. He wrote; it was for others to interpret.

It is customary and conventional for criticism to contend that, unless a writer himself is clear about what he wishes to communicate, his readers or his auditors cannot reasonably be expected to be sure that they have understood him through his writing. His writing, although rooted in him, should, it is said, be objective. This attitude towards the output of a creative genius, or even a highly imaginative, experimental, and talented craftsman, simplifies the issue to the point of distortion and falsification.

There is seldom only one right interpretation. There are often many facets of a whole, and the individual who ventures upon interpretation is much more prone to recognize and to accept facets that harmonize with his personality or that his personality enables him to see and to accept as authentic than to discuss the Absolute which is not embedded either in creation or interpretation. The playwright can be taken by surprise by what the critic in the theatre sees or fails to see and to read into his play in performance.

Shortly before the Second World War Sean O'Casey was stung into sharp rebuke of critics and their criticism. His volume[1] has for sub-title: "A laughing look-over of what has been said about the things of the theatre by the English dramatic critics, with many merry and amusing comments thereon, with some shrewd remarks by the author on the wise, delicious, and dignified tendencies in the theatre today." His "Overture" begins: "The dramatic critics that we have here take themselves very seriously, which would be something to laugh at if the actors, producers, and playwrights didn't take them more seriously than they take themselves. I often wondered and wished that the managers of the theatres had seats that could be raised and lowered devoted to the critics, so that each could be raised to the elevation that fitted his status, and then we'd see what a funny little regiment the critics form." Later, be becomes reminiscent: "Some time ago, one well known in the journalistic world, who is also a playwright, had a play produced which was adversely criticised by the critics. He rang me up and complained bitterly that the critics had done him wrong, insisting that the play had what the critics said it had not. I suggested that he should answer the critics back, and fearlessly point out where he thought them to be astray. He couldn't do that; oh no, he couldn't do that; such a thing wasn't done, and there was the end of it. (I had a big suspicion that he thought that I might do it for him.) 'They decided to slate the play,' he moaned, 'and I'll have to take my gruel without complaining'—and he complaining bitterly all the time—to me! The truth is that he was simply afraid to tackle them. If a dramatist hasn't an answer for the hope that is in him, then he isn't any great shakes in the Theatre."

In another chapter, "Mr. Ervine's Cry for the Critics," provoked by a special article published in *The Observer*, when St. John Ervine was the contributor of challenging essays on drama and the theatre, he stated: "Not so long ago in an

[1] *The Flying Wasp.*

article . . . Mr. St. John Ervine asked us among other things to believe that critics were honest; that though they cluster like bees on a first night of a play, they do not act in unison (as if we didn't know that already); and, really, that one critic is hardly known to the other (oh, come now, Mr. Ervine). Strangely enough, though the article seems to be concerned with the dramatic critics, their jobs and their virtues in their work, Mr. Ervine floods his article with instances of the critical or personal opinions of many well-known men, some of whom have or have had very little to do with the theatre. To prove that critics are honest and above any influence that friendship may have upon them, he tells us that Edward Garnett in letters to John Galsworthy habitually criticized Galsworthy's work, and that H. G. Wells, Granville-Barker, Gilbert Murray, W. H. Hudson, and Joseph Conrad (all of them creators themselves, equal to, if not greater than Galsworthy himself) did the same. These are fine names and anything they might say would be worth listening to, even though the advice given could not be accepted. Because Mr. Galsworthy thought their opinions worth having he asked for them, and gave them welcome, though some of them were bound to be unfavourable, for no clever writer can be wholly in agreement with another."

Playwrights are not alone in their disagreement with what some critics in the theatre write about plays, players, and performances.

The producer who has done his best, in accordance with his own interpretation of a play and with the players upon whom he must rely to fulfil the author's intention, may accept the adverse comment of the critic in the theatre as enlightened constructive criticism. As a human being first and a sensitive interpreter professionally, he is more likely to convince himself that his interpretation is right and that the blemishes in the critic's appraisement are the results of purblindness, of perversity, of inability to see how the different components of the production were, so the producer might think, dove-tailed most skilfully into a perfect whole.

Putting a play on the stage as the playwright may visualize it is the producer's task. The playwright *ought* to be able to visualize his play, written for the theatre, in terms of theatrical production, but he cannot always function in accordance with this particular "ought." Then the difficulty of the producer's task is increased, although, given a free hand, he may succeed better without aid than when the dictatorial influence of the playwright who doesn't know is inescapable.

Actors and actresses, too, are sensitive creative artists. If they have understood the playwright's intention and obeyed the producer's direction, they will be displeased rather than pleased by printed criticism of their contribution to the public performance, especially when seemingly they were popular and effective with the members of the audience. Some of the players who are resilient to every instruction of the producer, and who have worked in the theatre for years, will have become accustomed not only to respond to the producer's wishes but also have acquired confidence in their ability to meet them satisfactorily, knowing that their technique is adequate to enable them to register any desired effect. Others, and notably "the stars," fill positions of acknowledged privilege, their creative acting incorporating what technical mastery can give and also that elusive "something extra" which distinguishes the technically competent from the "born artist," whose technique in application, nevertheless, is often in need of the producer's control—hence the direction of West-End "stars" by producers of outstanding talent and artistry.

Shaw, as usual, was pertinent in comment. Writing "From the Point of View of a Playwright" as a contribution to a volume of memories[1] he stated: "The function of the actor is to make the audience imagine for the moment that real things are happening to real people. It is for the author to make the result interesting. If he fails, the actor cannot save the play unless it is so flimsy a thing that the actor can force upon it some figure of his own fancy and play the author off the stage. This has been done successfully in several well-known, though very uncommon, cases. Robert Macaire and Lord Dundreary were imposed by their actors on plays which did not really contain them. Grimaldi's clown was his own invention. These figures died with their creators, though their ghosts still linger

[1] *Herbert Beerbohm Tree.*

on the stage. Irving's Shylock was a creation which he thrust successfully upon Shakespeare's play; indeed, all Irving's impersonations were changelings. His Hamlet and his Lear were to many people more interesting than Shakespeare's Hamlet and Lear: but the two pairs were hardly even related. To the author, Irving was not an actor; he was either a rival or a collaborator who did all the real work. Therefore, he was anathema to master authors, and a godsend to journeymen authors, with the result that he had to confine himself to the works of dead authors who could not interfere with him, and, very occasionally, live authors who were under his thumb because they were unable to command production of their works in other quarters.

"Into this tradition of creative acting came Tree as Irving's rival and successor; and he, also, with his restless imagination, felt that he needed nothing from an author but a literary scaffold on which to exhibit his own creations."

"The Actor's Magic"

W. A. Darlington hit upon a worth-while theme for his book,[1] dealt with it interestingly, and, as an expert should, provocatively, with a natural preference that harmonizes with accepted first principles.

He obviously enjoyed turning again history's pages in order to present some of the pageantry that is inseparable from imaginative consideration of the lives of great players, in his particular case Burbage and Betterton, Garrick, Mrs. Siddons, Kean, and Irving. His chapter "The Actor's Magic" states: "We have seen six players who, each in his own time and before his appropriate audience, have come nearest to complete realization of the tragic actor's highest ambition—to wring men's hearts. In themselves they were people of widely different character and method; but seen at close quarters with one another they have likenesses more striking, and . . . infinitely more important, than their differences. Any speculations based on their dissimilarities must be fruitless, but if we consider the characteristics which the great players had in common we may possibly arrive at some conclusion not purely

[1] *The Actor and His Audience.*

academic; though whether by such methods we can hope to
put together a composite portrait of the Great Actor is more
than doubtful."

What makes the Great Actor? Mr. Darlington replies:
"Certainly the Great Actor need not be very much to look at,
at any rate to the casual eye . . . may be of almost any shape
of body or cast of countenance; but all the evidence goes to
show that he will have one remarkable feature—his eyes."

But the Great Actor need not have a specially captivating
voice: "All we can postulate of the Great Actor's voice . . .
is enough flexibility to make it able to express his emotions as
well as his meaning, and enough volume to make it as audible
as he wishes."

Is there any other common physical attribute? Yes. These
great players had strength—not the spiritual force there may
be in a puny body, but "plain ordinary muscular power and
control."

Having filled in illuminating details of a composite portrait,
which the author does not pretend has revealed a great deal—
"except for the remarkable and expressive eyes, it might stand
for a great footballer just as well as for a great actor"; also "it
may serve to dispel any lingering notion that the great actor
need have anything at all in common with the film star"—he
asks, in effect, What next?

The answer is the great actor's mental and spiritual qualities.
The author realizes and faces up to difficulties. He has no
wish to be called upon to explain the inexplicable. Therefore,
he selects a firm jumping-off place and avers: "The first
mental quality that the actor needs is the power of make-
believe, or, if you prefer a more dignified term, a creative
imagination." Any other qualities? Yes, first concentration—
or what Gordon Craig called single-mindedness in Irving's
case. And then "that individual magnetism which serves as a
shop-window for character, and is today usually called
'personality'." This, with "the capacity for ferocious hard
work which goes with it," takes people with talent and physical
stamina to success in their selected profession—"but the artist
must have more of it than most men because of the solitary
nature of his work, and the actor must have more of it than

most artists because his solitary work must be carried on in the midst of distractions."

Is, then, the answer to the question "What is the Great Actor's secret?" complete? Mr. Darlington doesn't think it is, for if the actor has no more than "creative imagination, concentration, and personality" he is not necessarily great. What will be lacking? The suggestion is "the power, possessed by the great player and by the great player alone, to establish between himself and a responsive audience a complete emotional accord."

Some members of the audience are inclined to turn themselves into amateur critics in the theatre—after they have been inside a theatre for an evening's amusement. They are entitled to their own opinions, which, in the majority, are in all probability as sincerely held as any that are formulated on a particular performance. It is improbable that anything the critic in the theatre writes will cause them to modify their own judgments of a play, the players, or the broad and general effects of the performance. Who is right? If the critic contends that a naturalistic play became artificial in the third act and there are differences of opinion on the point, whose judgment is to be accepted? That of the playwright who wrote the play in accordance with his ideas? If the critic states that an actress evidently misunderstood the character she had to portray, and the statement is not evidently acceptable to some, who must be blamed, the producer or the actress? If the critic confesses to boredom because a "thriller" repeats yet again all the technical tricks of the trade and the audience is "held" throughout by the recurrence of "manufactured" thrills, whose reaction is nearer the true valuation of the production and performance as theatrical entertainment, that of the bored critic or that of the excited and satisfied average theatregoer?

Members of an audience are indifferent. Their first impressions are probably synonymous with their lasting impressions.

" 'In the theatre,' Arthur Hopkins once wrote, 'I do not want the emotion that rises out of thought, but thought that rises out of emotion'." This will probably have its echo in the appreciation or appraisement of a play by the average theatre-goer. His or her emotional reactions can, in usual circumstances, be created much more readily than intellectual reactions on the level of the dialogue of a play of ideas, and spiritual reactions may spring from the virility of a deep-rooted faith that baffles scientific analysis. ". . . before we can learn how to die" Ramsden Balmforth points out:[1] "we have to learn how to live. In that sort of education, drama—and especially the modern drama—may be a great help. For while the ancient drama and the mediaeval mystery-play made the spectator merely an onlooker of the actions and sufferings of men struggling in the hands of the higher powers—Fate, Nemesis, the gods—the best modern drama (especially the drama of Ibsen, Shaw, Galsworthy and others, the drama of discussion and personality) makes the spectator a part of the drama—a creative personality, for good or ill, in the making of life and the ordering of the spiritual forces which determine the destiny of the soul."

The critic in the theatre who knows his job, and loves it, does not expect to receive unanimous endorsements of his opinions and judgments. He is conscious of the handicaps that the conditions of his theatregoing impose. Preliminary announcements may suggest to him the desirability of undertaking research work or of looking up references so that essential details can be garnered or memory refreshed. And the time-lag between the final curtain of a public performance and the latest time for him to hand in his criticism may give him respite for mature reflection, but he will not have abundant leisure before he commits himself to paper. At best he must be relatively quick, reaching decisions by which he must stand —or he must modify them in the light of criticism and his work.

To theatre notices and the manner of their production, C. E. Montague, one of the brilliant brigade of the *Manchester Guardian*, referred, in characteristic style, in his "Prefatory Note" to what remains one of the best volumes of reprinted dramatic criticism, *Dramatic Values*.

Is criticism that is the outcome of the presence of the professional critic in the theatre worth while? Has it value? Is it

[1] *The Ethical and Religious Value of the Drama.*

helpful? Reliable? Of interest to the average theatregoer who, turned "critic," often disagrees with the published criticism of the professional? A contribution to literature? To entertaining reading matter? To the evolution of drama or the advance of the theatre?

How easy it is to ask questions! Some can be answered by an actor criticized during his long career because of his own faults, the producer's misdirections, and the playwright's shortcomings. Quoting his own Press notices "to show how difficult it is to learn from the critics when no standard of dramatic criticism is possible," Ernest Thesiger, the actor-author, wrote:[1] "The painter is judged by his painting alone, the novelist by his book, the musician by his music, but the actor inflicts his own personality upon the audience and critics alike, so that it becomes impossible for them to say whether the performance is a bad one, or the personality of the actor antipathetic. There are certain critics who always praise certain performers, and others who invariably blame them. This can only mean that they are incapable of judging the work of the actor without being influenced by the reactions caused by his personality. One critic was honest enough to write once 'I never like Mr. Thesiger's work,' meaning, of course, that he couldn't bear the sight of me. That is quite understandable, but criticism should be a more impartial affair than that, and the critic above personal prejudices. The fact is that criticism is at once too easy and too difficult.

"I once became a critic. When I was wounded, a certain editor, out of the kindness of his heart, asked me to write some reviews for his paper. I protested that I was not literary and couldn't criticize books. 'What we want,' he explained, 'is the view of the man in the street, and you can present that view as well as anybody.'

"But if criticism is merely a record of the opinion of the man in the street it will benefit no one, except the cultured young undergraduate, who will find an easy job—plenty of them have —and make pontifical pronouncements about an art of which they know less than nothing. But the critic has, or should have, a higher responsibility than that. From whom else is the

[1] *Practically True.*

actor to learn, and to whom else can the public look for education?"

The contribution of the critic in the theatre is straight-forward, but it can be made only by scrupulously observing the severity of the conditions that the theatre imposes. The maintenance of professional reputation is of less importance than adherance to intellectual honesty. I do not suggest that the two are incompatible or impossible. Status, when compared with the fundamental value of truth to self, is secondary. A keen interest in activities that are expressive of the world's drama and of the theatre, sympathetic understanding of the aims of others, ability to see the present through the past and to glimpse the future—these are some of the attributes and qualities of the critic in the theatre.

Human institutions adapt themselves to contemporary needs with tortoiselike slowness. The critic in the theatre helps to accelerate the pace of progress in the theatre as a social institution when he keeps himself well informed about theories, methods, styles in playwriting, producing, acting. His enthusiasm impels him to make additions to his special knowledge and his sincerity induces him to apply it with unwavering integrity.

SOURCES AND BIBLIOGRAPHY

Extracts from the following works are quoted on the pages shown against each. Acknowledgment is made to the authors and publishers concerned.

AUTHOR	TITLE AND PUBLISHER	PAGE
AGATE, JAMES	*The Amazing Theatre* (Harrap, 1939)	107
AGATE, JAMES	*Ego 5: Again More of the Autobiography of James Agate* (Harrap, 1942)	19
ARCHER, WILLIAM	*The Old Drama and the New* (Heinemann, 1923)	26
BALMFORTH, RAMSDEN	*The Ethical and Religious Value of the Drama* (Allen and Unwin, 1925)	151
BEERBOHM, MAX	*Herbert Beerbohm Tree* (Hutchinson)	147
BENTHAM, FREDERICK	*Stage Lighting* (Pitman)	98
CELLIER, FRANÇOIS AND BRIDGEMAN, CUNNINGHAM	*Gilbert, Sullivan, and D'Oyly Carte* (Pitman, 1927)	97
CHARQUES, R. D.	*Contemporary Literature and Social Revolution* (Martin Secker)	13
CHURCHILL, R. C.	*Disagreements* (Secker and Warburg, 1950)	139
CORRY, P.	*Lighting the Stage* (Pitman)	99
DARLINGTON, W. A.	*The Actor and His Audience* (Phoenix House, 1949)	107, 148
DRINKWATER, JOHN	*The Gentle Art of Theatre-Going* (Holden, 1927)	111
DUKES, ASHLEY	*Drama* (Home University Library, Williams and Norgate, 1926) (now pub. Oxford University Press)	23
E. F. S.	*Our Stage and Its Critics* (Methuen, 1910)	133
ERVINE, ST. JOHN	*The Organized Theatre* (Allen and Unwin, 1924)	43
	Oscar Wilde (Allen and Unwin, 1951)	45
FINDLATER, RICHARD	*The Unholy Trade* (Gollancz, 1952)	11
GALSWORTHY, JOHN	*The Inn of Tranquillity* (Heinemann, 1912)	63
GIELGUD, JOHN	*Early Stages* (Macmillan, 1939)	83
GILBERT, BERNARD	*King Lear at Hordle and Other Rural Plays* (Collins, 1922)	6
GLOVER, HALCOTT	*Drama and Mankind* (Ernest Benn, 1923)	137

AUTHOR	TITLE AND PUBLISHER	PAGE
TRUMAN, NEVIL	*Historic Costuming* (Pitman)	96
USTINOV, PETER	*Plays About People* (Cape, 1950)	117
WALKLEY, A. B.	*Drama and Life* (Methuen, 1907)	123
WHITE, EDWIN C.	*Problems of Acting and Play Production* (Pitman, 1939)	71
WHITWORTH, GEOFFREY	*The Theatre of My Heart* (Gollancz, 1930)	142

The reader's attention is drawn also to the following works—

AUTHOR	TITLE AND PUBLISHER
BENTLEY, ERIC	*The Modern Theatre* (Hale, 1949)
BIRCH, DOROTHY	*Training for the Stage* (Pitman, 1952)
CLURMAN, HAROLD	*The Fervent Years* (Dobson, 1946)
CORATHIEL, ELIZABETH H. C.	*Oberammergau and Its Passion Play* (Burns, Oates and Washbourne, 1950)
DENT, ALAN	*Preludes and Studies* (1942); *Nocturnes and Rhapsodies* (Hamish Hamilton, 1950)
ELIOT, T. S.	*Notes Towards the Definition of Culture* (Faber and Faber, 1948)
ELIOT, T. S.	*Poetry and Drama* (Faber and Faber, 1951)
GARDNER, HELEN	*The Art of T. S. Eliot* (Cresset Press, 1949)
GORELIK, MORDECAI	*New Theatres for Old* (Dobson, 1940)
JOAD, C. E. M.	*Shaw* (Gollancz, 1949)
LAWRENCE, GERTRUDE	*A Star Danced* (W. H. Allen, 1945)
MACCARTHY, DESMOND	*Drama* (Putnam, 1940)
NICOLL, ALLARDYCE	*World Drama* (Harrap, 1949)
PATCH, BLANCHE	*30 Years With G. B. S.* (Gollancz, 1951)
PEARSON, HESKETH	*G. B. S.: A Postcript* (Collins, 1951)
SEYLER, ATHENE and HAGGARD, STEPHEN	*The Craft of Comedy: Correspondence between Athene Seyler and Stephen Haggard* (Muller, 1943)
STANFORD, DEREK	*Christopher Fry* (Nevill, 1952)
TREWIN, J. C.	*The English Theatre* (Elek, 1948)
TREWIN, J. C.	*The Theatre Since 1900* (Dakers, 1951)
TYNAN, KENNETH	*He That Plays the King* (Longmans, 1950)
WARD, A. C.	*Specimens of English Dramatic Criticism XVII–XX Centuries* (Oxford University Press, 1945)
WILSON, A. E.	*Edwardian Theatre* (Barker, 1951)

INDEX